Here's to

Great Adventures

Health &

Happiness

Darel

Healing Journey

The Odyssey of an Uncommon Athlete

David Smith
With Franklin Russell

Sierra Club Books
San Francisco

The Sierra Club, founded in 1892 by John Muir, has devoted itself to the study and protection of the earth's scenic and ecological resources—mountains, wetlands, woodlands, wild shores and rivers, deserts and plains. The publishing program of the Sierra Club offers books to the public as a nonprofit educational service in the hope that they may enlarge the public's understanding of the Club's basic concerns. The point of view expressed in each book, however, does not necessarily represent that of the Club. The Sierra Club has some fifty chapters coast to coast, in Canada, Hawaii, and Alaska. For information about how you may participate in its programs to preserve wilderness and the quality of life, please address inquiries to Sierra Club, 530 Bush Street, San Francisco, CA 94108.

The names of all the Pioneer Program trainees, Earth House patients, and participants in the Blackwater Adventure Run, and details of some incidents in these chapters, have been changed.

LIBRARY OF CONGRESS CATALOGING IN PUBLICATION DATA

Smith, David, 1938 Oct. 17-
Healing Journey.

1. Smith, David, 1938 Oct. 17-   . 2. Athletes—United States—Biography. 3. Outdoor life. I. Russell, Franklin, 1922-   . II. Title.
GV697.S63A34 1983   796'.092'4 [B]   83-4754
ISBN 0-87156-804-7
ISBN 0-87156-809-8 (pbk.)

Jacket design by Paul Gamarello
Book design by Paula Schlosser

Printed in the United States of America
10 9 8 7 6 5 4 3 2 1

To the memory of my grandfather, William, who walked the length of wild America, and my father, Seymour, who taught me the value of wilderness

To the spirit of my son, Daren, who walks in the wilderness with trust

David Smith

Acknowledgments

Many people helped me to organize and carry out the adventures described in this book. Some are named in the text, others not, but to all of them go my deepest thanks.

A few individuals need to be mentioned by name for their friendship and support: Frank Calhoun and Wayne Villeneuve, both of whom worked on the Blackwater Run; Judith Fairchyld; Rick Field; Emile Lacampgne;   Corine Lorain; my old scoutmaster, the late Arthur Meyer; and Ed Muckerman.

Other friends who read and commented on the book in various stages of manuscript include David Brink, Bill Harvey, Judy Lynn, and Mack Shealy.

My literary agent, John Boswell, worked on the concept of the book with me and has been a faithful supporter throughout the long process of its creation. I thank Jon Beckmann, director of Sierra Club Books, and Diana Landau, my editor, for their faith in the idea and patient guidance during its execution. Freelance editor Linda Gunnarson expertly shaped and trimmed the final manuscript.

My very special appreciation to the following people:

Robert Jones, senior writer for *Sports Illustrated*, for his creative input on several adventures.

Rosalind LaRoche for giving me the chance to use wilderness activities with the patients at Earth House.

Producer and director Fred Levinson for his friendship and the use of his New York apartment to work on the book.

And my family—my mother, Gladys; my late father, Seymour; my wife, Rebecca, and our children, Daren and Chelsea; and my brother, Jay, for their constant encouragement and patience with my frequent absences from home or from the country.

Finally, I thank my collaborator and good friend, Franklin Russell, who found a way to put words to this story and whose friendship, though tested many times in the process, I value as much as his literary contribution.

David Smith

Contents

Preface

Embarkation

When David Miln Smith was thrown out of a university for the second time, he started thinking. He was drinking a lot, and he was gambling. He lived for good times—for parties, pretty women, and handsome cars. He assumed that he could do just about anything he wanted. He owned a popular, trendy San Francisco bar and had a large group of friends.

But there was a lot to think about. He had put on weight since he had stopped swimming competitively. He was in such poor shape that he puffed when climbing stairs. He was not sleeping well. This state of things was ultimately unacceptable to someone who, at the age of twelve-and-a-half, had achieved the distinction of being the youngest Eagle Scout in the world; someone who had been a high-school swimming champion; a young man whose father, a prominent San Francisco surgeon, had expected him to enter one of the professions.

"I knew that I had disappointed my father," says David, "but when I thought more about it, I realized that I had disappointed myself even more."

In the spring of 1964 David began to change his life. For six months he struggled to find a formula that would break his patterns of behavior. "I was never sure what I

1

wanted," he says, "except that my life had to be different."
As an athlete his instinct was first to put himself back together
physically. He stopped smoking. Then he wondered whether
he could, in fact, stop drinking. All his friends drank. Drink
was the lubricant of social life. Could he have any fun without the booze?

He knew, very certainly, that the gambling had to go.
He was not an especially heavy player; but he was a regular,
and he lost more than he won. And he knew that his diet of
starchy and junk foods had to change if he was to pull his
body back into shape. Bad food and physical fitness simply
did not go together.

Gradually the change took hold. Then, rather suddenly,
its pace accelerated beyond his expectations, and its scope
extended beyond physical conditioning to the beginnings
of an altered state of mind. The booze went. The gambling
ended. He found himself swimming again with the enthu-
siasm of a kid, gliding through the water like a champion
reborn. He made some spectacular long-distance swims that
attracted worldwide attention. He sold the bar and his fancy
cars. At a certain point he felt the need to test himself in
deeper, more distant waters, and he set out alone with a
pack on his back to find a new way of life. The story of that
remarkable journey is the subject of this book.

The literature of the human species is rich with stories
of transforming change. As long as change is possible, there
can be hope. And with hope there is energy. The ability to
change is our greatest asset. Unlike other species we do not
have to wait around for millennia for the slow evolutionary
alterations in behavior and form that environment demands.

But change means steps into the unknown, and the
human animal—all animals—resists change because it is
usually frightening. Profound change can require us to
abandon our entire infrastructure of memory, history, and
belief. When David Smith turned his life around, he entered
a strange new world indeed. He felt possessed by a force of

nature that made him a kind of superman, enabling him to
do things that were beyond his measured capabilities.
Eventually he came to call the agent of his transformation
"the source." But obviously there was no adequate word to
summarize the extraordinary change that had overwhelmed him. "Each time I try to describe it, the damned
thing falls apart," he would say ruefully.

Sometimes he would feel that he was merely fine-tun-
ing his body. Everything came out right because he had
trained, and then willed his body to perform. At other times
he was certain that some external force was responsible for
his enhanced performance, tireless energy, and endless
optimism. It sounded flaky or corny, even to himself, so he
kept his mouth shut on that score. But there was unques-
tionably a special kind of elation he had never experienced
before, an ecstasy that spilled over into everything he did.

From this elevated state of mind he conceived and carried out a series of unique athletic adventures, using the
wildernesses of the earth as his settings, his arenas. He swam,
walked, ran, climbed, kayaked, parachuted, and bicycled—
usually in places where no one had thought to do such things
for any reason other than survival, often among people to
whom his presence and endeavors seemed little short of
madness (although perhaps of a sacred sort). More sophis-
ticated observers, such as the news media, found David's
adventures entertaining and frequently newsworthy, if not
much more. But for David himself they were primarily
opportunities to explore this phenomenon he called the
source. Was its power a separate energy, or just his own,
enhanced? Was it sprung from his discipline of effort, or
did it come from the environment? Was it a force of the
wilderness? Although urban-based, David was a wilderness
child, partly reared in California's Sierra Nevada by his
outdoorsman-physician father, and he absorbed the wilderness as a stimulant, an energizer. Did the source heal?
There were more questions than answers.

When David first came to me with a preliminary manuscript in hand, written partly by him and partly by a journalist friend, his message was contained in its title, "The Healing Wilderness, A Journey of Self-Discovery." This was in 1978. I advised him that his message, although fascinating, did not easily yield to words. "It seems to need music," I said, slightly facetiously. I underestimated the man. He would spend a thousand hours persuading me that the story of his journey should be told.

The wilderness he had written about contained a spiritual element akin to Emerson's moral nature, in which there was a correct way to think and behave. For Emerson, nature released the energy of thought. It helped restore a primal balance of self. For David Smith, the wilderness released the suppressed potential of the body to perform astonishing feats. But at the same time it re-created a more innocent notion of action, where truth and honesty and decency invariably triumphed over evil. And that, of course, was the real problem of his manuscript. Who could believe that stuff?

Finding the source in nature seemed too simple a solution to the complexities and paradoxes of life. You became fit. You ran or swam through the wilderness. Your troubles were over. Yet there was compelling evidential support for David's working thesis that the natural environment could energize the athlete. Anybody who has worked in a dirty, dark factory knows about the negative power of environment. There was no doubt, from my own experiences, that the solitude of nature, the true wildernesses, always had a stimulating effect on the human mind.

The immense blue dome of the Australian Outback sky is not the same stimulus as the moaning wastelands of Antarctica. There is a distinct difference between standing on the summit of Kilimanjaro and trudging through Death Valley. The giant sentinel icebergs of the Arctic speak another kind of message. But there is a common language to these places. It can be heard by anyone and understood by those who take time to translate it.

There is an abundant literature describing the relationship between humanity and the natural world. Thoreau's musings on natural history are evocative, but they have more to do with humanist philosophy than with the deeply mystical nature of the woods. David Smith's experiences parallel Thoreau's intellectual genius in reaching the source of nature. But Thoreau could not combine the intellectual with the physical and so could not put the energy to work in his body. He died prematurely, in his forties.

Going deeply into the source implies a return to a primal state. David is something close to an animal in his marathon swims, his trancelike meditations, his exposure to the challenges of nature. I am reminded, looking at his exploits, of a wolf running down its prey. There is simply no sign of fatigue in those limber legs. They cycle on, hour after hour, the rib cage expanding and contracting with easy breaths, the whole effort bespeaking inexhaustible energy.

Primitive people have the same physical competence and grace, the sense of being in place in their world. Both David and I have lived with men and women close to, or in, the Stone Age. Neither of us are believers in the notion of the noble savage, but both of us have walked trackless, waterless deserts with such people and have seen how it is possible to drink when there appears to be no water, to eat when there is no game in sight. We have lost touch with such abilities, but David Smith in his adventures recalls them, and our past, to us.

He talks of an altered state of consciousness. But perhaps this is something closer to the original state of human perceptions and capacities. The source energizes the body to perform without conscious effort—a kind of automatic volition—like playing the piano at the point of no longer having to think before striking a note. Ten fingers and two feet coordinate with eyes rapidly scanning a page of complicated hieroglyphs, the music pouring out with almost limitless variation in feeling, speed, and expressiveness.

Nijinsky used to say that when he was dancing, it was like watching someone else perform, seen from the orchestra pit. As David Smith demonstrates and has experienced, it is not uncommon for athletes to have "out-of-body" experiences in which they can actually see themselves swimming or running or climbing from some vantage point beyond their own bodies.

The source is implicitly moral. It is right action, at the right time, in the right place. To me, this is an astounding perception. David has come to exactly the same conclusion as Emerson, a formidable intellect who puzzled for years over the language of landscape. The energies of inspiration are implicit in wilderness. The Bible is full of examples of those who went into the wilderness and came back transformed, with the word of God in commandments, with the knowledge of how to save humanity. Both Jesus and Buddha turned personal experiences in the wilderness into insights for all.

The great mythologist Joseph Campbell believes that any journey into the wilderness is a mythic act of heroism. The traveler goes out to and returns from a dangerous place, bringing back wisdom for the benefit of others. Each of David Smith's adventures is a heroic journey with a moral. As a tiny figure kayaking along the vast, sinuous length of the Nile, he battled the fear of the unknown, drinking in the mystique of the desert. He ran down Fujiyama to enact the hero's descent from the clouds and ran a marathon around a volcano in Hawaii to symbolize man's conquest of the fear of fire. He has acted out almost all his ideas and fantasies and has passed along a lot of them to others.

It took David and me a year to find out that his story did not work in any single philosophic context. Finding a voice was a problem, too; I tried for another year to write his message in the third person. But I kept separating myself from the essential connection that he had to the source. I assumed that the task was to describe a power uniquely his, rather than everyone's power to tap into the source and thereby change their lives.

David never lost patience with me. He lives by the principle that nothing is really impossible. He was a dropout but came back into society. He is a critic of convention, but he does not believe in revolution. He is an optimist about the worst aspects of human nature and, unlike most exemplars, makes no claim to having sure-fire answers to anything.

"I just have experiences," he says.

David's genius is that he has transformed the hero's journey into everyone's experience. Though his adventures may be exotic, the insights gained by them apply to all of our life journeys. When he swam the near-freezing waters of the Hunza River in the Karakoram Range, he demonstrated that true contentment comes as a result of risk, discipline, and dedication to principle. He did it in such a way that a hardy Himalayan mountain people applauded him for his toughness. But earlier, on the other side of the world, a group of young schizophrenics had applauded him for his gentleness and generosity.

When the United States reached its peak of affluence in the mid-1960s, when David Smith himself was reaching adulthood, a small band of citizens began fleeing from "the good life" as expressed in materialism. Affluence, their thumping feet and sweating faces were saying, has no spirit. It does not generate growth or insight. It tends to be self-serving. There is no ecstasy in indulgence, only satiation.

By the end of the sixties a trickle of joggers had grown to a small stream, people who nodded to each other as they passed in public parks, like conspirators in a plot to overthrow the reigning consciousness. This was the period when people laughed at David Smith as he ran down Park Avenue. By the end of the 1970s the stream of joggers had turned into an Amazonian flood of millions of runners, jumpers, swimmers, walkers, parachutists, rock climbers, backpackers, kayakers, and cyclists—the greatest mass explosion of voluntary personal energy ever seen on earth.

It did not matter that many of these new runners were knock-kneed or that they shambled rather than ran. Eighty-year-olds ran alongside teenaged women; families, lovers, husbands and wives, youth clubs, insurance clerks, salesmen, and baseball players all ran together. Speaking with their feet, quite ordinary people made a profound statement about change, inspiration, action, and identity. They demonstrated a new truth in American life. "Winning" did not necessarily mean coming in first. Nobody even glances at David Smith running down Park Avenue today.

Yet although all these people are basically seeking the same state of euphoria that David describes in this book, it is not easy to attain. The search is a journey, an expedition, that can only succeed when many requirements are met. The source cannot be experienced at all unless a successful and sometimes painful return journey is completed. There must be some danger, though not necessarily physical. There must be an excitement of escape, a sensation of being healed, a feeling of deep change.

Now a tidal wave of humanity reaches for David Smith's source, by whatever name they call this phenomenon. For most people, it is a blind, intuitive reaching for a better way of living. They may suffer considerable pain. Certainly they understand the meaning of physical deprivation as they face that endlessly unreeling pavement, those last few pool lengths.

However, David transforms this striving for self-improvement into fun. He has a sense of humor. He swims the wrong way in a race in the Mediterranean, then shrugs when he ends up in Pompeii instead of Naples. He is gored by a bull near Malaga but understands that his vanity upended him, not the bull. Through all his expeditions his message is clear and without cant, and he delivers it time and time again. If I have gotten it down right, then his expeditions to the source should be amusing; yet behind them lie profoundly urgent messages of insight and wisdom.

In trying to help David express himself, to bring his story out of the metaphysical jungle that often shrouds this kind of inspirational experience, I have overstretched the bounds of a collaborator. I have overlaid the story in places with my own interpretations and perceptions of the phenomenon that he is trying to enact. In that sense the book is written by me.

But David himself is the "source" and center of the story. It is due to his energy, his drive, his wildly creative and implacable insistence, that it is being told at all. He knows the source like few other men, because he is both athlete and thinker. He has come down from the sky under a parachute with his message and has emerged from the ocean deeps with it. In this sense the book is entirely his.

Franklin Russell
New York City

Chapter 1

Swimming the Golden Gate

It was a typical San Francisco evening. The bay waters sparkled in the setting sun, and a great blank wall of fog lingered beyond the bridge. From my car, parked on a bluff overlooking the Golden Gate, I watched the scene with a friend, an interesting and attractive woman named Judy Hall, who had once been Miss Utah. As we sat watching, the fog slowly advanced toward the bridge, consuming all visibility in its path. The tide was turning. At the same time a Matson liner was in the middle of a tidal rip that often runs down the center of the channel. We could see the waters dancing upward along the hull of the ship, throwing up little dashes of foam. Hundreds of passengers were looking down into the turbulent waters.

"That's a really spectacular sight," said Judy. She loved the sea.

The foghorn on the Golden Gate Bridge began blowing. Automatic-flashing amber lights flicked on before the fog reached the structure. We could hear the rush of waters in conflict. The fog swallowed the ship section by section until only the thunder of its foghorn told us it was still there.

"Damn!" I said. "I'm going to swim the Gate!"

"Don't you have to be in shape for that?" asked Judy.

"You have to be in terrific shape," I said.

11

Judy was a good friend. She was both practical and imaginative, and she sometimes acted as my conscience. I listened to her when she talked about the kind of life I was leading. Earlier that day she had suggested that I was frittering away my time and wasting my talents.

"I don't see you as a bar owner and a man who throws his money away at Lake Tahoe," she had told me.

"What am I, then?" I had replied. "I own a bar, and I play the tables at Tahoe."

"You could be somebody who contributes to society rather than just taking enjoyment from it. Somebody important."

"What's important?" I asked her. "You mean straight, square, supporting the war in Vietnam, that kind of important? Look, I win money at golf. I've got a roomful of swimming trophies from school . . ."

"I'm sorry," she had said. "I'm really sorry I mentioned it."

But she had struck a nerve.

The truth of it was that I was really fed up with myself. How could I describe it? I had everything—a thriving business, plenty of money, and a lot of close friends. I could do pretty much anything I wanted to do. In my bar, the Dirty Bird, located in the Richmond district of San Francisco within easy access of a dozen college campuses, a huge mural dominated the wall behind the old, scarred wooden bar. It was a picture of Hollywood's "Rat Pack"—Dean Martin, Sammy Davis, Jr., Frank Sinatra, Peter Lawford, and Joey Bishop—all dressed in Egyptian costumes and carrying a litter high over their heads. I lay contentedly on the litter, also Egyptian-clad, and grinning down at my patrons. "This is a fun place," I might have been saying.

But I had become edgy about where all the good times were taking me. I was getting tense about all the drinking, the parties that seemed to go on forever, the fact that I was smoking a lot and eating too much. I kept letting out my

David in his twenties. SUZY BAXTER.

belt and saying that I would go on a diet soon, but I never seemed to get around to it.

I knew, then, as I sat with Judy by the bridge that evening, that if I went through with my plan to swim the Gate, I would have to take a long journey backward. I would have to return to the days of athletic training, when excruciating hours were spent gaining tiny improvements in speed and endurance. But it also was becoming clear to me that I wanted to go back even farther than my days as a competitive swimmer, back to the times of my childhood and teens, when my father had taken me every chance he got into the Sierra Nevada mountains.

One of the great features of the Sierra Nevada are the many thousands of small lakes, or tarns, scattered throughout its rocky system. They are encountered unexpectedly by the impulsive traveler, but my father and I knew the location of hundreds of them. We would tramp along together by the banks of a stream tumbling down a river canyon, with cliffs and spires of stone rising around us, imminently about to reach a "yosemite," a broad valley of waterfalls. Invariably we would come upon a lake. My father would rest. I would swim.

My father had a deep understanding of almost every aspect of animal and plant life in the Sierra, and he loved to share it. I learned everything from bird calls to wildflower identities. Once, he, my younger brother Jay, and I were backpacking through some giant sequoias, with shafts of sunlight filtering through the foliage high overhead and gleaming on banks of lupine blossoms and crimson snow plants. My father stopped us with a gesture. "See how the idea of a garden was invented in nature," he said. He was full of spontaneous observations. Another time a chipmunk was hunched down in a hollow log, bathing in a fine dust of sequoia bark, which, my father said, was impregnated with tannin. "It acts as an insect repellent," he told us.

The mountains were essential to him. Without them, he said, he could not handle the load of his medical practice in the city. "Up here," he would say, sitting in front of the log cabin fire, "is where I get put back together again."

His father, William, was born in Ireland the same year as John Muir, 1838, exactly 100 years before me. He came across the United States in a covered wagon with a wife and four children. His wife died. Years later he remarried, to an Englishwoman. She had a son—my father—born when my grandfather William was sixty-four years of age.

David in Yosemite, on a return visit to the Sierra Nevada in the mid-1970s. JOHN HIDALGO.

I grew to share my father's love of the mountains. While one part of me was engaged in the noisy, friendly, exciting city, another part was most content in the deepest solitude of the Sierra. Even as a youngster I noticed the terrific difference between living in the city and in the mountains. In the city I was all nerves and energy, but in the mountains I settled into a serene, cool state, in which I felt my batteries were being recharged for the return trip down the highway, through Sacramento and back into the city.

I hadn't been to the mountains much in recent years, and I had grown apart from my father, too. It was probably not too different from a lot of father-son relationships in those days—mine had worked his way through Stanford Medical School and clearly was mystified and disappointed by my devotion to sports and indifference to academic achievement in high school, and especially by the feckless way I'd been conducting my life since then. A week after I had been kicked out of college for the second time—for a prank the local newspapers found worthy of mention—my father had attended a medical school reunion in which much of the conversation had revolved around the activities and accomplishments of the doctors' offspring. He hadn't had to tell them what I was up to. Neither of us was happy about the distance and bad feeling that separated us, but neither of us knew what to do about it. But I had reason now to think back to our times together in the Sierra, as I faced the prospect of abandoning the gregarious city life that I relished. I knew that if I were to train seriously for a Gate swim, I would have to remove myself almost entirely from society. I would be making a journey, an essentially lonely journey, into myself, in search of something that was meaningful to me alone. In that journey my friends would be my enemies, my enjoyments would be my liabilities, and the blandishments of society in general would be impediments to any change. I had to see life differently, yet I had mixed feelings about the new path I was taking.

But the Gate offered a focus, a place to make a beginning.

I had belonged to the San Francisco Olympic Club since I was ten years old, soon after I first showed swimming talent. I had done track work there, played on basketball teams, and swum at meets. I had won a lot of Olympic Club trophies over the years, but I had not swum in the club pool for seven years, about four years longer than I had owned the Dirty Bird.

The morning after my decision to swim the Gate, nursing a small hangover, I was at the Olympic Club when it opened. The pool was empty. I looked at it with a kind of dread. "All right, body," I said, "I hope you're ready for what's about to happen to you."

I dived in and swam two lengths, and it was worse than I had expected. I was completely blown. When I reached the end of the pool, I saw Bill Wilson, the club coach, folding up some collapsible chairs. "Hey Bill," I called out, "I'm going to swim the Gate, and I need to get in shape fast. What's the score?"

"When you can swim a mile a day easily," he said, "you'll be ready for the Gate."

That would be fifty-three lengths every twenty-four hours.

The secret underlying all training is the athlete's ability to inspire himself. He must hold on to a vision beyond himself. At least, that was how it had always worked for me. The body must sweat and the mind must be committed, in equal measure. It is not especially difficult to make the body perform difficult and tedious tasks. But if championship performance is the goal, then the training becomes almost wholly a discipline of the mind, with the body obediently tagging along behind the vision.

After a month of hard work I could swim a mile in the pool. It took much longer than I expected. But as I trained, I found myself recalling experiences from earlier swimming days. I remembered not the triumphs but the mistakes. One incident in particular ran through my mind. I would be making the Gate swim sometime around my twenty-sixth birthday; this incident had occurred a decade earlier, on my sixteenth birthday, when I decided to compete in a harbor race from Pier 7 in San Francisco to Treasure Island, a distance of about one-and-a-half miles. I figured this was a breeze for a sprint swimmer like myself.

I also thought I understood about cold. The water of San Francisco Bay is about fifteen degrees colder than the pool water in which I did most of my swimming. While this might prove to be a shock to my system, it would not be critical, I thought, because I already was acclimated to "dipping" in the Bay, which most San Franciscan youngsters regard as being full acclimation to cold.

I set out with great confidence and style, and all went well for about a mile and a quarter. But then, suddenly, the cold struck me with cramps in both thighs. I stopped dead, bobbing up and down under the Bay Bridge, which links the Berkeley-Oakland area and San Francisco. There was only about two hundred yards to go, but that was not the nub of my difficulty.

Before the race I had told my friends who would be in the pilot boat following me that I should not be rescued, no matter how much I might pretend to be in trouble. They understood about my practical jokes. But now, unable to kick at all, desperately bitten by the cold, I waved and shouted without effect. My friends were laughing at me, waving back and shouting, "You can make it, man! Just swim! You're almost there."

I went under once and swallowed a lot of water, and then I went under again. The third time my friends realized that I was truly in trouble. But the Bay currents can be quirky, and they found themselves caught in one running against them. They could not get the boat to my side quickly enough. By something just short of a miracle, a Coast Guard boat was passing nearby, and it veered and scooped me up just before I was about to take the last big swallow.

I had never thought of this incident, frightening as it was, as representing a fault in character. But now, in the enforced solitude of rigorous training, I was shaken by its revelation. I had been a youngster who, as characterized by one teacher, "lacks seriousness of mind." I had thought that winning every swimming race I entered was seriousness enough.

The great San Francisco experts in cold-water swimming were the members of the Dolphin Club, some of whom—mostly older men—had acclimated themselves to swim year round in the Bay. As I trained in the Olympic pool, I knew I must plan to complete my training in sea water. But more importantly I had to insure against any risk of cramps. The Dolphin experts emphasized how essential it was to be *accurately* acclimated to the cold water.

"The cold is deceptive," said one of them, Dan Murphy, who had swum the Gate a couple of times before. "You get used to it, right? You feel fine. You can stand the water for a couple of hours, but then, zingo! Down you go! The thing is this, kid. You've got to be able to stick out the cold *and* swim hard."

The place and the challenge were working on me. I began spending hours at Fort Point, just sitting on the sea wall or on the beach, watching the Gate waters. The Gate stimulated my preparation to swim it; in turn, my capability to swim it became the lure to go down there and just let its presence flow into me, an energy field that I was about to join.

Seen purely from the standpoint of the swimmer's strength, the Gate was a challenge of environment. It was a place of many conflicting currents, and the swimmer had to be strong enough to cope with their shearing collisions. Often when the tide was turning, a rip could be seen running down the center of the channel; Judy Hall and I had seen it dancing against the hull of the Matson liner. It appeared as a scar of whitened water, wavering under the bridge, as incoming water from the ocean raced past the outgoing water from San Francisco Bay.

The Gate was a theater of small dramas played out by the tides beneath the bridge. The low murmur of traffic high above was a reminder of the proximity of the manmade world, from which the swimmer, while in the water, would receive no help. One current curved like a broad horseshoe around the beach at Fort Point and plunged out to sea like a speedboat, throwing up drifts of spray. Its force was terrific. Occasionally when incoming ocean waves met the outgoing tide they would create steady, near-toppling ridges of energy that swept through the Gate and into the Bay. On some days surfers now ride these waves, letting the power of the Pacific carry them into the city.

When I got down to the finer details of swimming the Gate, I understood that I had two options. I could elect to swim with the outgoing tide and be carried along for about half the swim, until I met the rip, when I would face the incoming tidal waters. The risk was that I might misjudge my strength, or my resistance to the cold, or how far I had been carried, and be unable to fight against the incoming water when I crossed the rip line.

My second option carried much the same risk, but in reverse. I would strike the incoming water when I was fresh, and so could fight it strongly. But once I crossed the rip line, I would be in the grip of the outgoing tidal waters. These might, in my then tired condition, carry me beyond my capability to reach a fast-receding shore.

During my training I decided to practice with the Dolphin Club members and then join them in their annual Gate swim. I also became friendly with Ike Papke, a Hawaiian longshoreman who had achieved fame some years earlier by swimming from Catalina Island to Los Angeles, a distance of about twenty-six miles. Papke had become an ardent exponent of distance swimming as an expression of a person's will and identity.

"You've got to think about what you're doing, David," he told me. "You're a social animal, and distance swimming is a pretty lonely business."

I also got to know George Farnsworth, who had made a specialty of the Alcatraz swim and was in tough shape in his late forties. Frank Drum, the popular head of the Dolphin Club, became a friend. Drum was one of the few who completely understood what I was doing. "That Gate swim," he said, "has pulled a lot of guys together."

As the date for the Gate swim approached, I began to sense the group excitement as the Dolphin Club swimmers started to display their "highs" of readiness for the ordeal ahead. On the day before the swim I drove down to Fort Point. It was a beautiful morning—the sky clear, the waters

With George Farnsworth (left) and Ike Papke (right) the morning of the Golden Gate swim. SEYMOUR P. SMITH.

sparkling blue. I felt a great connectedness to the place, an eagerness to be in the water and in the grip of its immense power.

I also felt the tension of wanting to prove something about myself—to myself, mainly, but also to my parents and others. My mother had said she wanted me to "make a record of some sort, the way you did in the pool all the time." My father didn't say much—he didn't seem to know what to make of my suddenly revived passion for swimming, or maybe he was just reserving comment. But he did say that he would wait for me at the end of the swim.

The following day, when I wakened, it was miserable outside. Not only was the city buried in dense fog, but a chill drizzle washed all the streets to greasy black slicks. I called Papke, who told me that the Gate swim had been canceled. I told him I was going to swim anyway, but he persuaded me that the fog would make the swim both uncomfortable and problematic. "I need to see the shore when I'm leading you," he said.

A week later, this time in brilliant morning sunshine, I was at the shores of the Gate, accompanied by Papke and Farnsworth, who would be my pilots. Almost immediately an odd thing happened to me. Just after I got into the water, my body felt possessed by a strange feeling, as if tiny charges of electricity were running through the nerve endings. At first I attributed it to excitement—I had really wanted to get swimming. But the feeling was different from any high or excitement I had felt before. It flowed through me like a powerful guidance system.

As I Australian-crawled away from land, I thought I had been lucky enough to pick up a shore current that was helping me along toward the rip. But soon I realized that it was no current. It was some power inside me.

"Take it easy, David," I heard Ike Papke say from the boat. "You don't have to do it in record time."

But the feeling told me otherwise. It was a message. It said that nothing could stop me; I was going to "win." I felt no cold. The slaps of the waves, now whipped by a sharp wind sweeping under the bridge, filled my eyes with salt under the goggles. But all I felt was exhilaration. Instead of swimming in a daze, grim and determined, I was floating along in a crystal palace of the mind, remembering everything, knowing everything.

"Oh boy," I said to myself. "Oh boy."

With each stroke I expected to be let down, to be cold, to be struggling against the current. Instead I felt only an extraordinary focusing of effort, a compression of my whole being into a unity of action. What could it mean?

Dimly I recalled bits and pieces from Greek myths I had read, telling of the fire that burned inside a man's soul and that, when it was hot enough, made him almost god-like. It was the center of consciousness, the good and the bad suddenly working together.

Was that it?

The rip tide crest showed ahead of me, and I could feel the tug of waters beginning to urge me out toward the Pacific. Apparently I had misjudged the tide. I could see Papke gesturing, but I heard nothing. Suddenly I was in the rip, being torn in two directions at once, and within seconds I overturned completely, so strong was the shear of waters.

Then it seemed as if only about twenty seconds elapsed before I felt gravel under my palms, and I was in the shallows at my destination. I emerged from the water like a man in a dream.

"What is this?" I asked myself. "Am I going crazy?"

It felt so unreal. But it was also a high. I had never been so high.

People were all around me, clapping towels on my shoulders and slapping me on the back. I was with them, laughing and smiling, delighted with myself. But I was also apart from them, the possessor of some kind of secret that I felt I could not share because I certainly did not understand what it was about.

My father stood there, a bit back from the crowd. We shook hands.

"Good luck," he said. "You're on your way."

Chapter 2

The Pillars of Hercules

After the Golden Gate swim I had to take a long look at myself. Who was I in relation to my new-found strength and ability? I could explain my success in swimming the Gate—I had trained properly and was prepared to meet the challenge. What I could not explain was the exhilaration that had enveloped me in the water and the sheer effortlessness of the swim. It seemed to me that I had experienced an altered state of consciousness; this was obviously a gift that demanded, first, use and, second, investigation. But was I the only person to have experienced this feeling? Weeks after the swim I was still perplexed.

At first, right after the event, I felt as though I were high all the time. This was not like a sudden flush of energy that occurs occasionally and propels you to the top of a mountain or into a dancing jag or through an all-night party. This was an apparently continuous and different state of being. But what to do with it?

Clearly I must swim. Almost at once I learned that the world record for the twenty-four-hour nonstop indoor swim had remained intact for more than fifteen years. I started training, then broke the record by six miles, swimming forty-one miles in the twenty-four hours.

This was heady stuff. It earned some publicity, and I began to wonder just how far I could swim. When my father asked me about it, I said, "I have this weird feeling that I could swim forever." I was only half joking.

At about this time I saw a documentary entitled *The River* in a film class at the University of California at Berkeley. The film profiled the Mississippi River from source waters to delta. My imagination was caught; I could see myself swimming from Lake Itasca, in Minnesota, to New Orleans, a distance of more than two thousand miles. But first I had to find out whether such a swim was feasible.

I chose the Sacramento River, which flows through California's Central Valley and into San Francisco Bay, as being typical of the mid- and downstream waters of the Mississippi. In a test swim I completed sixty-three miles in the Sacramento and assured myself that it would be possible to swim about twenty miles a day for up to a hundred consecutive days. Then I tackled the swifter Russian River, in northern California, as representative of the headwaters of the Mississippi. I swam thirty miles in that test swim.

But it seemed I was ahead of my time; certainly it was way beyond the capability of potential backers to believe that the swim was possible, or that it would be the spectacular event I envisioned. I tried to line up sponsors, but none of the sports equipment manufacturers could see it as either practical or glamorous.

In an interview for a California television station I tried to relate the Golden Gate "feeling" to the possibility of the superlong Mississippi swim, but the interviewer cut me off. After the show he gave me some advice. "Steer clear of the metaphysical stuff," he said. "The audience doesn't want that kind of 'reality.' People want entertainment and escape. They want you to do what they don't have the guts or the strength or the ability to do themselves. You're their agent in adventure. But for God's sake, you're not the person to suggest that they may be missing a way to a better life."

A well-known California public relations expert described the fault of the Mississippi idea. "It's a fabulous idea, as a feat," he said. "But it has no class in TV land. What's the Mississippi to the TV watcher? A bunch of old paddle-wheelers and some boring floods in places nobody ever heard of. Now, if you'd do the Amazon! Man-eating fish! Blood-thirsty natives in dugout canoes! You'd get sponsors for that."

Instead of being discouraged I did some research. Was there a swim that had never been done?

There was indeed. Despite repeated attempts nobody had ever swum the Strait of Gibraltar, the so-called Pillars of Hercules, from Africa to Europe. Many had gone from the southern tip of Spain south to Morocco, but the swim northward had defeated scores of good swimmers.

It was one thing to conceive of such a swim and quite another to plan it from the United States. While making preparations I tried once more for a sponsored swim, this one coinciding with a transportation strike in New York City. I would swim across the East River from Brooklyn to the island of Manhattan, in the January cold, as a means of celebrating the individual spirit being demonstrated by millions of New Yorkers who were getting to work despite handicaps. The swim was scheduled, but as the media people were waiting for me to slip into the water, the strike was settled.

I stayed in New York and trained in an indoor pool at a Brooklyn hotel during part of that winter, and then I wangled a crewman's berth on a Norwegian freighter to Europe. I hitchhiked to southern Spain and immediately met a remarkable Gibraltarian, Horace Zammitt, who understood exactly why I wanted to make the first south-to-north crossing of the Strait. Ebullient and high-spirited, Horace was a sergeant of police and a former long-distance swimmer who devoted his spare time to helping swimmers seeking to conquer the Pillars.

"Your swim idea is terrific," he said, "but there is a problem. It is impossible."

One man, a talented Irishman, had made seventeen attempts to swim north, and Horace had watched him fail each time.

"You need a lot of speed to beat the main current," said Horace.

"Maybe I've got the speed," I said.

"And you must have the stamina as well," he said.

As part of my training and to convince Horace that I was both serious and fast, I arranged to swim across the bay that separates Algeciras, on the Spanish side of the bay, and the harbor of Gibraltar, about seven miles away on the British side. I crossed the bay in two hours, which was a medium-distance pace, almost a sprint, for a long-distance swim. After the swim Horace invited all of his friends to a party, and in the middle of it he made a toast: "I want you all to toast the man who I think will, at last, be the first to swim the northern route."

I said nothing about the powerful feeling I had had during the Golden Gate swim. Indeed, I had no better handle on it. There had been no sign of it during the twenty-four-hour swim, even though I had swum tirelessly, won a city golf tournament three hours later, and then gone dancing. None of my training swims for the Mississippi project had produced a similar feeling. I was starting to think that, having experienced the feeling and been changed by it, I would not feel it again. Yet I was puzzled, because my intuition said that it was *supposed* to come again.

I went to Morocco to begin training with a San Francisco Dolphin Club member, Bill Sakovich, who was coaching the national Moroccan team in his work for the Peace Corps. I swam in the pool at the national sports complex in Rabat. When I wasn't working on speed in the pool, I did distance training in the Bouregreg River and rough-water practice in the Atlantic. Once during a thirty-five-kilometer swim in heavy fog I blundered into an artillery range of the Moroccan Army. The place must have been a jinx because the next year, at the same spot off the Moroccan coast, I was chased out of the water by an eight-foot hammerhead shark.

"You'll need some help on those currents in the Strait," said Bill. "I don't know anything about them. They're worse than the Gate, I'm told."

I hastened back to Gibraltar, where I found a group of smugglers who knew the tides and currents the way a taxi driver knows the streets of a city. Though all were convinced that the swim was impossible, one of them, whose name was Carlos, offered to serve as chief pilot in my small flotilla of boats.

"The weather is important, too," he said, tapping his forehead, "and I will advise you on that."

Carlos briefed me on the currents as we left Gibraltar for the Moroccan starting point, a beach named Punta Ceres about twenty kilometers east of Tangiers. Altogether there were five currents to consider. Two currents ran in opposing directions along the African shore, but Carlos did not see them as a great problem. "You will make it through them because you will be fresh."

But the main, east-west current was another matter. This powerful central current flows east, into the Mediterranean, on the surface, and then ebbs west, into the Atlantic, about fifteen feet below the surface. The greatest problem occurs with the surface flow; it is so strong that it pulls you farther and farther into the Mediterranean and away from the Iberian Peninsula. To successfully cross the Strait, therefore, it is not possible to swim the shortest distance shore to shore. Instead, as the smuggler Carlos knew from experience, the swimmer had to time his journey to enter and make use of the surface and subterranean currents as best he could.

Preparing for the Africa-to-Europe swim. ENRICO SARSINI,
Life, © Time, Inc.

Finally, on the European side of the Strait, there were
two more conflicting currents to cross, a few miles offshore.

When I stood on the beach at Punta Ceres, facing the
small boats bobbing in the inshore swell, I felt nothing except
a supreme, almost arrogant confidence that this swim was
going to be a breeze. I was wearing only goggles, a swim-

suit, and bathing cap, according to the contest rules of the English Channel Swimming Association, and I would be swimming in a shark cage, as stipulated by the Gibraltan government. Giving the British victory sign to my supporters—Horace, Bill, and Carlos—and the news media, I plunged in where the shark cage lay mostly submerged and entered it.

I can't imagine there is anything more daunting to any person of accomplishment than to discover that everything in which he or she believes, and has come to trust and rely on, is wrong. In the first two hours of this swim the previous twenty-four months of uplifted experiences and high expectations were totally demolished, and I began to suspect that I'd been a victim of my own hyped-up optimism. I was ready to quit before I was even five miles away from the Moroccan shore.

The trouble was pain.

Any athlete—and especially a distance swimmer or a marathon runner—is familiar with pain as a consequence of great effort. There are ways of cutting down its impact, by training properly and by easing up to "highs" of performance rather than crashing through to them in great bursts of energy. But the pain I was experiencing in the Pillars of Hercules made me feel as if my body were possessed by classical demons straight out of a Greek myth. It was pain that seemed malevolent, pain designed to stop me rather than just warn me that I was stressing my body too much. And, most dauntingly, it was pain before it was expected, pain without sensible cause, paid before I had even begun to put on the effort that would push me through the big central current.

At first I thought some of the pain was caused by the nausea that developed after sea water slopped into my first feeding of Coke syrup. Then I thought it came from dehydration. I'd been unable to keep down the Coke syrup or tea and glucose, and lack of fluids certainly impaired the body's functioning. My throat, swollen from the constant drip of sea water, burned and stung as I continued to throw up in the choppy seas. At this rate it seemed there was no way I could finish the swim. It was a very bitter moment.

I felt as though red-hot pokers were being pushed into tender tissues—shoulders, elbows, chest—and I wasn't sure at times whether I was throwing up from seasickness or the pain. Desperately I invoked my favorite tricks for setting the pain at bay. I dreamed. I fantasized. I hallucinated. I concentrated on trying to recapture the feeling I had had swimming the Golden Gate. But I felt nothing except pain. "I will not let up," I told myself, "until the pain goes away. I will move with the pain, I will endure it, I will outlive it." I had a simple mantra to repeat: "Strength-stamina-determination."

The pain went away for a bit.

After the Gate swim I had learned to flip my arms forward with a special jerk of the shoulders, a very hard action at first—breaking an athletic habit is about as hard as quitting smoking—but which, when mastered, gave me improved speed and better endurance. Then, as the arms flipped forward and bit into the water, I felt as though I were skidding across the surface with little effort. But here in the Strait, when I flipped, each arm was enveloped in white-hot pain as it cut into the water.

Something was radically wrong. Had I been fooled by the Golden Gate feeling? Was it all an illusion? Perhaps all this pain was a sign that I was biting off more than I could chew. All the Gibraltarians had told me it was impossible. A madman's dream. It occurred to me that I might be a bit crazy for refusing to believe them. Was there such a thing as overmotivation?

Perhaps I blacked out. I had no memory of crossing the big central current. But Horace's roar penetrated the fog of pain: "Coast in sight!"

My mantra came to the rescue. I stuck to it for another two hours. Suddenly, it seemed, the shore near Tarifa, Spain, was two hundred yards away. Horace and Bill jumped into the water and began swimming alongside me. My chest felt as though it would cave in. My palms struck rocks. I staggered ashore seven hours and thirty-five minutes after I had walked into the water off Africa.

Horace's voice came again, unforgettable: "Congratulations! You're the first bloke to do it!"

But the only thought in my head was that I was going to die. Then Horace's voice came again, very faintly: "I hope he doesn't die."

That was the last thing I heard before I crashed down on the rocks and passed out.

Then: "Who are those guys?"

"Guardia! Get him up, get him up!"

"Come on, David. There are two soldiers with guns running down the beach. You've got to make the boat, man!" The Guardia Civil did not applaud illegal entries into Spanish territory.

"I can't do it, Bill."

"Think of this. Five years in a Spanish jail."

"I could rest."

"Breaking up rocks, lying in your own filth. No sleep, ever!"

They dragged me into deeper water and I managed to flounder back to the pilot boat. The rope to the shark cage was cut, and we surged away from shore to the accompaniment of angry shouts and waving arms by the two Spanish militiamen.

The huge party that followed in Gibraltar was an international event. It was crowded with press people who had gathered to cover the first swim from Africa to Europe. The champagne toasts, the applause, the snapping of electronic flashes, all occurred in front of a man who was barely present, scarcely able to focus. I grinned and waved and responded "appropriately." But inside I was a mess.

Before the crowd my exterior voice said, "It is a great honor and privilege to be here with you all." But my interior voice said, "I thought I'd tapped into the source of the earth's energy, but now I feel like just another swimmer."

I had to remind myself that I had made a record-setting swim. But such pain, such complete contradiction of the Golden Gate feeling. Later I leveled with Horace as best I could. But of course he could not feel what I felt.

"Don't worry," he said. "You take a big rest, and you will feel fine again."

The director of tourism, Manuel Serfaty, had another idea.

"Next year," he said, "you must do the swim again, but this time arrive in Gibraltar, and you will come ashore among friends."

The idea was so outrageous it made me feel sick. But it did raise the all-important question of what I should do next. Swim again? Quit? Go back to San Francisco? How could I face the press there, applauding me for a "victory" when I felt so utterly defeated? I needed time to think.

I went up the coast to Malaga, participated in a bullfight in a privately owned ring and ended up back in Gibraltar, in the hospital, after being tossed by the bull. I remembered the move I had seen a matador make while fighting in Pamplona, Spain, in 1960; I had been there to join in the famous running of the bulls through the streets. He had faced the bull without his cape, or *muleta*. At the exact moment, he had stepped out to the side with his right leg, at the same time shifting his weight to that foot. It was like a fake in basketball. The bull had veered to the matador's new "position," and then the man had shifted his weight quickly back to his left leg. At the same time he moved his right leg out of the way of the bull's horns. His leg was, in effect, the cape.

I copied the movement exactly, but I missed the last step. I had been thinking about the move rather than making it. Later, as a Gibraltar doctor drained blood from my injured knee and recommended an operation, it came to me in a rush. During the Strait swim I had been thinking about the triumph of arrival instead of summoning the energy that should have made the swim "effortless" and satisfying. My mistake, it occurred dimly, was in some way connected with my focus or intention.

I did not take time to think this idea through, though. Instead I had some hazy idea that if I could just do enough swims, I would connect again with that effortless energy manifested in the Golden Gate swim. Thereupon followed a summer of almost complete madness.

Still limping, I entered an international swimming race from Capri to Naples, twenty-five miles and forty swimmers from all over the world. I swam fast and well, and there was very little pain, and I made headlines in Naples after the race. Unfortunately the publicity was not because I had rediscovered the energy source I was seeking, but because I had arrived in Pompeii instead of Naples. I swam twelve-and-a-half hours in the wrong direction. When I was interviewed, I said that my boatman must have been in the pay of the Mafia. Nobody laughed.

The Mediterranean is steeped in myths and legends. I realized I had been influenced by them, in part, to swim the Pillars of Hercules, "conquering" the gateway to the classical world. Perhaps I could find my power source by imitating, or joining, the ancients.

I decided to swim the legendary waters of the Hellespont—now called the Dardanelles—that long, current-driven strait that separates Asia from Europe. A girl friend, Kathi Bohanna, came with me. Once again my focus was on achieving the goal, on completing the swim, as the key to rediscovering the power I sought. It would be a while yet before I realized the fallacy of this.

The legend surrounding the Hellespont was compelling. Leander, a mortal, had glimpsed Hero, a goddess, at a picnic of the gods and thought he had discovered the source of all happiness. But he could not explain to anybody what it was like to love a goddess. His affair with Hero had to be clandestine. Nightly, guided by her lamp, he swam the Hellespont to visit her, until one night, in a storm, he drowned. Hero, who had discovered her own source of joy in the love of a beautiful mortal, cast herself into the stormy waters and drowned too.

The poetic significance of this myth caught the imagination of the English poet Lord Byron, who found in the story (told in many poems from the Alexandrian period) a source for his own imagination. He swam the Hellespont in 1821, in three hours and forty-five minutes.

From Istanbul Kathi and I took a bus seven hours south and then a boat across the Dardanelles to the Asiatic side of the strait; we looked out across the water from pretty much the same point from which Leander and Byron had left. It was a real letdown. I don't quite know what I expected, but it seemed so banal—a row of waterfront bars and cafes and a rocky beach.

"Somehow," I said, rather bleakly, "I just can't get excited by the idea of Hero waiting over there on the other side."

"She wasn't waiting for you," said Kathi.

"Well," I said, "maybe you could go over there and wait for me."

"I don't want to act like a goddess," she said.

"Well, I don't want to drown, either," I replied.

The Pompeii disaster had made me determined to get only pilots who knew their way, but I could not find anybody who "knew the currents." Eventually I had to almost drag a fellow out of a waterfront bar, just because he could row and had a dinghy.

"But you don't know whether he has any notion of the currents, or anything," said Kathi.

I shrugged. "I was really hoping for a better atmosphere," I said.

"You just don't dig Turkey," she said, climbing into the dinghy.

I jumped into the water just in front of the bar. Omar, the boatman, a bald guy with a mustache and arms like a wrestler, bent his chunky body to his tiny rowboat and spun it away from the shore.

"You must going against current," he said. "This way!"

He pointed toward Russia, or so it seemed to me. Actually the European shore was only a mile away, and the houses, shops, and roads were clearly visible from the Asian side. It did not look like much of a swim at all. Why had Byron taken so long to make the crossing? More to the point, why had Leander *drowned*? Whether he had lost sight of Hero's light or it was the worst storm in history, the fellow had been swimming this stretch of water every night to be with his lady love. It seemed to me that I'd have to be attacked by the Turkish Navy to fail this swim.

So I was not exactly exuberant as I got going in the water. Right away we ran into technical difficulties. Kathi kept directing me to the northeast, acting on instructions from Omar. I kept resisting, pointing toward that nearby shore, which, after ten minutes of swimming, looked almost close enough to make a sprint for. But then I started to feel the pull of the current. This was the great outflow of the Black Sea, compressed into the Bosporus a hundred miles north, then racing south into the Sea of Marmara. There it slowed, only to pick up speed again here at the Dardanelles, where I was swimming.

Soon I wasn't arguing with anybody. I was just struggling to keep my heading toward the farther shore without being carried south. I understood then how Byron had been swept toward the Aegean and why his swim had taken nearly four hours. I knew why Leander had drowned here. He had been trying to swim it alone, without a boatman, and at night, with only his lover's light to guide him. When the storm came down on him, he had no reference point, no light. He was swimming blind. He drowned because without a perceptible destination he was nowhere. His energies were wasted in the darkness of the sea. I made the other shore in a little more than forty minutes; then Kathi and I rode the bus back to Istanbul. I had been in my wet swim trunks for seven hours, and I was simmering. It had seemed like such a good idea, but now I was mad at myself. Instead of getting closer to the source of that effortless power I was seeking, I was about as lost as Leander.

Clearly there was no point in just blindly swimming onward in the hope that I would stumble into the Golden Gate feeling again. The only thing that made me unique—in my own mind at least—among the hundreds of capable distance swimmers performing internationally was this mysterious fountainhead of energy, this "source." It came to me then that I was not seeking some symbolic achievement or trick of energetics, but an actual place, an environment of specific power, within which I could function as I had at the Gate. By so envisioning it as an environmental rather than as a psychic power, I believed I had made a big step toward rediscovering it.

I decided to make one last swim that summer as both a test of the search and also, perhaps, as a finale to the long-distance swimming that was failing me so completely. The Egyptians were staging an international swimming marathon along the Suez Canal. I joined it with Cliff Lumsden, the famous Canadian coach who had trained Marilyn Bell, the first person to swim across icy Lake Ontario. The canal, however, was the temperature and consistency of warm milk. We swam at four in the morning, behind an enormous floodlit picture of Nasser that was towed on a barge. I drank twenty-nine Cokes. Lumsden pulled out after three hours. I kept chugging along, but when the sun came leaping up out of Saudi Arabia, I thought the canal was going into a low boil. I was about to quit when my palms suddenly began hitting the bottom. I was perhaps half a mile from the shore, in the Great Bitter Lake, one of the large stretches of water linked by the Suez Canal. I swam for another few minutes and could have finished the race, but I stood up in that ridiculously shallow water and shouted for Lumsden to throw me another Coke. This was no environment in which to experience anything serious. I stood in water up to my knees and began laughing.

The fact was that we had been treated sumptuously in Egypt, feted as international heroes in street parades and at receptions, and there was no way I could reconcile this luxurious and public atmosphere with my very personal, almost spartan, quest for an elusive feeling. The Suez swim was, in truth, the antithesis of what I sought.

I had begun the year determined to expand my experience of altered consciousness. But most of the swimming had been just hard work, and the Gibraltar swim had been dauntingly painful. I discovered nothing on that swim that any marathon swimmer did not already know.

I returned to San Francisco in the winter and began reading everything I could lay my hands on about altered states of consciousness, personal transformation, and spiritual and metaphysical experiences. I hunted for examples of the effects of environment on the psyche. There was a lot written about mystical experiences, which could be interpreted in many kinds of ways. I read about the ecstatic states reached through singing, dancing, war, and sexual love, and about esthetic ecstasy produced by the contemplation of elegance, the beauty of objects and art. And, of course, there was the ecstasy of swimming.

It became apparent from both my experience and reading that one of the most vital elements leading to spiritual uplift or transformation was the isolation of the individual in a remote environment. There it was possible for effort to become fused with identity because of the lack of outside interference. It was clear also that any complete focusing of physical effort—or any intense effort—produced dramatic changes in both performance and perception. There was "a wealth of the inner world" available to the seeker, as one text described it. Furthermore, there was no single track, no single destination, no single experience of ecstatic feeling. It was a million journeys, as varied as the people who chose to make them. But it must be true that they all functioned from that common source I had hypothesized late that past summer.

I discovered *siddhi*, the Hindu word for spiritual power that could produce extraordinary control over the body, the feeling, the thinking, and other mental functions. I began practicing yoga and meditation to direct my intuitive drive for transforming change.

However, it was in an old maxim—which I knew long before I began reading—that I found the clue to the disasters of my swimming in the Mediterranean. It dealt with the difficulty of "becoming" when you strove too hard to "become." It said: "A mind burdened with becoming can never be tranquil, for tranquility is not a result either of practice or of time."

By striving I pushed the objective away.

There was an absurdly simple way of testing my conclusion. Manuel Serfaty, in Gibraltar, had put the idea in my head. I would re-enact the swim, but this time I would head for Gibraltar itself. And this time, if my hunch was correct, I would slip back into that powerful feeling of the source, and I would laugh across the waters that had made me scream before.

Horace was ecstatic to see me again when I arrived in Gibraltar to make the European arrangements for the second swim.

"You will land among a thousand close friends," he promised.

In return I promised myself to forget that this swim was still considered "impossible." Most Gibraltarians, it

Approaching Europe on the second swim. ENRICO SARSINI,
Life, © Time, Inc.

seemed, remained skeptical. "The marathon swimmer, David
Smith, was lucky to slip through the currents in his 1966
swim," editorialized one of the British newspapers.

Early one morning I walked down the Moroccan beach
at Punta Ceres, the point of departure for the first swim.
My small flotilla of boats was lined up offshore. The new
shark cage was a bit better than last year's model; the
Gibraltarians had dug up some commercial-quality mesh.
A shark might take about ten seconds to get through this
cage.

Suddenly I laughed. I felt no anxiety about success, no
focus on destination. I just felt drawn into the water. The
sea embraced me, buoyed me, and the waves cradled me.
There was no nausea, and I did not expect too much pain.
When I raised my arms out of the water, they seemed to fly
forward and take giant bites out of the water. My kick wake
hissed behind me.

"Steady!" shouted Horace through his megaphone. "We're not chasing records, David. You're already the champion!"

It made no difference. The state of effortless energy was upon me, unbidden, but there in a great flowing force that made it almost impossible to slow myself. The athlete is always grateful whenever vastly improved performance comes upon him, when he is literally performing beyond his perceived ability. I had read story after story about this during my winter of research in San Francisco.

I was leaving Africa in my wake, but whatever this feeling was, it had nothing to do with winning or pulling off long shots. I could even feel a strong, strange connection to the Rock of Gibraltar, a magnetic and compelling presence. It was just a matter of time and distance before I got there.

But the swim itself was not a swim as I had experienced it before. It was instead a peace. Pelé, the great Brazilian soccer player, described a similar feeling when everything went right for him in a soccer match. He felt "a strange calmness I hadn't experienced in any of the other games. It was a type of euphoria; I felt I could run all day without tiring, that I could dribble through any of their team, or all of them, that I could almost pass through them physically. I felt I could not be hurt. It was a very strange feeling and one I had not felt before. Perhaps it was merely confidence, but I have felt confident many times without that strange feeling of invincibility."

Instead of journeying to Gibraltar, I was immersed in a journey that led only to the place where I already existed, in the water. This was the place! The sea smoothed itself into a great welcoming embrace. I flew toward . . . where? It didn't matter. The currents fell away. A German freighter passed close by, and the flotilla people shouted and cursed. We had to do a 360-degree turn to avoid ramming the ship, but I was like a machine, swimming through the freighter if necessary. I felt myself at the threshold of another break-through, another change.

It felt as if the very molecules of the Strait's waters were combining to ease my passage. I knew this was in my imag-ination only, but if this were truly a combination of the environment and the swimmer within it, then perhaps I was charging the waters around me with my own energy. Or the energy of the water was charging me. It really did not matter which way it was, as long as the source of the power kept sweeping me onward.

Suddenly this image of the physical and the meta-physical gave me a feeling of negative and positive, of good and evil; it might be expressed as demons and angels by a storyteller dramatizing his material. I had angels with me now, but demons had been present. I knew them from the first Strait swim. As I moved in concert with the energy upon me, some code of behavior or attitude or cognition was being broken, steadily smashed to pieces. I was moving effortlessly because I was free from the fear of what the demons might do.

At the end of the seventh hour—just about the time I had staggered ashore in Spain the previous year, after cov-ering thirteen miles—I had swum twenty-four miles. I was within sight of Gibraltar. I had crossed the Strait in a vast arc, at first swimming toward the Atlantic and then allow-ing the incoming current to carry me past the coast of Spain. I had not really fought the current this time. I had merged with its power and made it my own.

"You're swimming awfully fast, David!" shouted Horace.

The man who is flying beautifully does not think about landing. He knows it is the flying that is important, not arriving at the airfield or even returning to earth. He has transcended himself and has put himself in touch with the infinite. In this moment I felt a universal power—the source of all energy—passing through me. I was open to it, and I became its channel. Later I discovered that the people in the boats felt it, too.

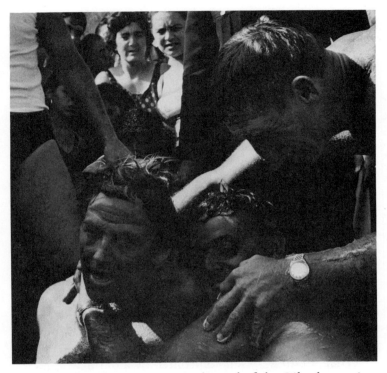

A victory hug from Horace at the end of the Gibraltar swim.
ENRICO SARSINI, *Life*, © Time, Inc.

Instead of reducing my effort I seemed to increase my speed. I could hear Horace shouting occasionally, almost pleadingly, but I paid him no attention. I was averaging more than eighty strokes per minute, up from sixty the year before.

The great rock loomed up to my right as I came into Algeciras Bay. Yachts, motor launches, and outboards were beginning to leave the shore, and many were decorated with welcoming pennants. Soon they were flanking me, and the British thumbs-up sign surrounded me. I felt like Sir Francis Chichester coming home after circumnavigating the world in his tiny yacht.

As we came toward the beach where we had planned my landing, about two miles distant, Horace jumped into the cage to complete the swim with me. "But first," he said later, "I put on flippers, so I could keep up with your speed."

To the Gibraltarians I was a hero, and that was okay. But I had made two journeys. There had been two identities in action between the Pillars of Hercules. One was acting for the external world. It gave the performance, mastering a difficult task and reveling in the triumph of arrival. But the far more important identity was interior. I had invented a quest for the source of this mysterious power, a quest I shared with nobody else. That journey was as invisible as the great submarine current that swept the waters of the Mediterranean back to their source in the Atlantic, beyond the Pillars.

As the cage was lowered, Horace and I sped free of it, and I rose up the beach, with Horace dripping behind me. He was ecstatic, bear-hugging me so hard that I collapsed, gasping. The newsreels and photographs in *Life* magazine showed later that I did not, in fact, look so good. But inside I was glowing.

Then, finding myself confronted by a battery of microphones thrust into my face, I made what must have been the most baffling remark in Europe that day.

"What do you know?" I said. "I'm not just a swimmer anymore."

Chapter 3

Across the
High Atlas

In 1960 the thriving port city of Agadir, located on the Moroccan Atlantic coast about three hundred miles south of Casablanca, was leveled by an earthquake. It was one of the most devastating earthquakes of the twentieth century, and indeed of all time, rivaling the great Lisbon destruction of the eighteenth century. There was literally nothing left standing in the city. Forty-eight thousand people lived in Agadir; 12,000 died in the earthquake.

On this midday in the fall of 1968 I trudged out of the town of Marrakech, under the brooding invitation of the High Atlas Mountains to the southwest. Before me lay roughly three hundred miles of desert, foothills, mountains towering more than 12,000 feet, a precipitous plunge to the roasting sands of the Sahara, and then a great emptiness of dune and stony plain leading to the shores of the Atlantic and my destination, the completely rebuilt city of Agadir.

After the first Pillars of Hercules swim I had been hired to appear in a Camel cigarette commercial in Marrakech. (It was for the "I'd walk a mile . . ." series, a slogan that turned out to have a certain irony in my case.) I had been in the uproarious camel market, filled with grunting, blatting, squealing animals. Suddenly, between two camels'

Checking out the local transport, near Marrakech.
LEE MARSHALL.

heads, I caught a glimpse of the snow-clad High Atlas Mountains, like a mirage suddenly visible in a choking desert. I knew then that whatever the outcome of the second Gibraltar swim, my next adventure would be on land, perhaps in those mountains, perhaps in the Sahara itself.

I came out of the second Gibraltar swim determined to continue the journey in search of the source of whatever it was that I was experiencing. I wanted the mountains or the desert to speak to me in the way that the water adventures had spoken, to see whether in those great land-blocked silences of dune and stony plain I might not tap into a different kind of energy leading to another place, another change.

The first fifty miles of the journey took me from Marrakech to the foothills of the High Atlas and plunged me into a totally strange environment. This stretch of desert was a great, aching, brown and gray void. It offered no comfort to the strange traveler. Instead it suggested another kind of contact, its hostility a mask for the fact that there were people who had made these dry places their own— people like the fabled Tuareg Blue Men I had read about, who forged from their environment a cultural identity so strong that ordinary Arabs, used to such hot, dry places, stood aside in deference to them.

Nearing the foothills, as I passed through olive and orange groves, I began to sense the kind of change this environment could effect in me. I felt I was exploring the outer limits of my understanding. I watched a cluster of burnoose-clad figures—Berbers—waiting in the shade of a large rock set against the sweep of rising foothill. Were they dangerous, friendly, asleep, or just disinterested? I saw a man, his arms raised, chasing a small boy from a turreted mud house; was he going to hit the little boy or hug him? Then I saw him, Lilliputian in the distance, bring a big, flat rock crashing down on the child's head. The boy fell, and I started forward with a shout, sure that I had witnessed a murder. But the child got up. Then some teenagers started throwing rocks and olives at me until I was out of range.

I had read about the Berbers, called "lords of the Atlas." They are a fiercely independent people indigenous to this part of North Africa, with their own language and culture. When the tough French Foreign Legion took over Morocco, they couldn't capture the High Atlas—the Berbers living there were tougher. An adventurer who had spent years alone in wild places told me that the Atlas walk was ill-advised, partly because of the Berbers: "You could get killed for breaking a custom you never knew existed." At the very least, he said, pack a gun.

Each evening during my journey the sun went down so swiftly that it seemed about to crash into the rocks on the horizon. The second day out, still in the foothills, I groped through the suddenness of nightfall until I found a camping place in a niche among towering rocks. Before leaving Marrakech I had decided to observe Ramadan, the Moslem month of fasting from sunrise to sunset, which had started some days earlier. I had not had food or water the entire day and found myself savoring a simple supper of whole-wheat Moroccan bread and dark, aromatic tea. Within minutes after eating I was asleep.

From the foothills I took a meandering course and wandered through some of the valleys of the High Atlas. These valleys lead the traveler inward, toward the snow, and are unlike any other landscape I have ever seen: winding, graveled rivers glittering under Moorish ruins rising from bleak slopes, tiny villages set into curves of shale and rock, dwellings that appear to grow right out of the earth. There is no way of knowing exactly how long the Berbers have inhabited this place, except that there is a feeling of immense antiquity, and of conjunction, man to mountain. I walked swiftly but in a friendly fashion, greeting the people I met with sufficient reserve to allow them to be friendlier if they so chose. The Berbers are courteous, but I was told in Marrakech that a Berber would as likely rob or kill me as take the time to greet me or offer travel directions.

One man—an elder of Asni, a mountain village—indicated in a vigorous pantomime that it would be too cold for me farther up in the High Atlas. He also tried to describe other dangers. He pretended to seize a man's head in his right arm and to plunge an imaginary dagger into the chest and the belly. I felt a chill. Most of the people I met in the mountains would use this pantomime. Mustapha, a Moroccan I had met in Marrakech, had performed it for me a dozen times.

Mustapha had noticed a small transistor radio that I had bought in Gibraltar, and he said, with the peremptoriness characteristic of many Arabs, "You give me that radio." I said I wanted to use it out on the desert, since I would surely be lonely out there. But he insisted that I give it to him immediately.

"Now, now, now!" he cried.

"Wait, wait, wait!" I said. "Tell me first what you want
it for."

"My father doesn't have much money," he said. "He
cuts hashish all day, and it would nice for him to have the
radio. It would be good for him."

"All right, Mustapha," I said. "When I come back, I'll
give it to you."

"No," he implored. "You give it to me now. I tell you
true!" He had tears in his eyes. "I tell you real true. You
crazy. You never come back. You get killed in mountains
by Berbers."

I kept moving steadily higher into the High Atlas. Alone
all the time, the voices of Marrakech rang in my ears. In
the aching silences I could hear a kind of thrum. Was it the
desert calling to me? It was easy for the imagination to
work overtime here. The gloom of each gathering night was
a challenge.

And the cold. The mountains were freezing. The moon,
striking down on such bleakness, enhanced my evening
apprehensions. I remembered the man at the Moroccan
tourist office who had said to watch out for mountain cats.
I had to stifle the thought of some primitive cat out there,
stalking me.

One evening I concentrated on reading a small book by
Lucretius, a Roman poet who had been thinking thoughts
similar to mine in the first century B.C. "There is no disorder or anxiety of man," he wrote, "that cannot be cured
by a detailed examination of the workings of nature. They
alone provide the answers that men seek. They alone can
give us a cure for the disorders of the mind."

Before the desert or the mountains could speak to me,
I had to try to understand their language. I was caught in
an extraordinary journey of new perceptions, a renaissance
of feeling. My tiny stick fire helped warm my shivering body,
and I used a characteristic Arab gesture—a toss of the arm
and a twist of the body—to adjust my djelabah more tightly
around my body. Beyond the flicker of the fire, the vast,

empty spaces of the Atlas, the spare and lonely rivers, lay brooding. When I lay back against a tree and watched the empty sky, I felt such an absence of people that it was almost painful.

Yet in Marrakech I had looked at the mountains and felt their presence like a magnet. The people there—in the Medina, the marketplace—knew how to deal with desert and mountain. They polished copper and brass underneath masses of hanging wool that they had dyed bright orange and yellow and black. The metal, the woven cloth, the shapes and colors, all spoke of the place where I now crouched over my tiny fire. The atmosphere of the Medina spoke of camels and travel in the days before tourists and four-wheel drives.

In the evenings there, waiting to begin my walk, I had sat at rickety wooden tables with beggars, drinking mint tea. One fellow, toothless and half blind, told me that smoking kief (a narcoticlike drug made from hemp leaves) made you crazy and certainly caused your teeth to fall out. He also said the desert was a friendly place, where the Berbers would help me every step of the way.

Marrakech is a place of storytellers, and I loved that, because I realized by then that I was acting out my own life story. The storytellers gathered large crowds around them in the square, where they spun their long and complicated tales. One man sat on a rug about fifteen feet long, surrounded by the sum of his worldly possessions, and told stories to a blind man who sat at the other end of the rug. The blind man would jerk his bald head up and down; a tuft of hair growing out of one side of his head like a big feather made him look like some strange kind of bird. The two men would spin story after story off each other. Every day I would sit on the rug and just listen, even though I did not understand more than a dozen words in Arabic. Somehow most of it got translated in the mind. I was learning that by giving myself over to an environment, the place itself then spoke to me, the language became comprehensible.

In this way desert and mountain must speak to me, and I would understand.

The mountain cold was deceptive. During the day the broken-up rocks stored heat and radiated it, so that I could feel heat coming from the clear cool sky and also from all around me. I could not touch many of the rocks. But the moment the sun disappeared, the temperature really took a dive. One night around sunset I threw down my djelabah for a few minutes—I was sweating—and took in a magnificent view of desolate peaks, plunging river courses, and ruins standing in medieval isolation from each other, all of it empty of humans. When I picked up the djelabah, which was lying now in shade, it was frozen. I had not brought a tent, and this night I would need shelter.

I was in pretty good shape. But cold is especially dangerous to the finely tuned body that is not also hardened to temperature changes. You're more prone to cramps when you're in good shape. I didn't want to get cramps up here, alone on top of a Moroccan mountain.

In the far distance a geometric shape showed itself against the dying colors of the day. I could see that it was a building. Shivering, my muscles stiffened by the cold, I went toward it. It turned out to be a great old Moorish ruin that must have been put up before Columbus reached America, a square structure with several floors still intact. The place was freezing. My sweat turned to ice in my sweater. I tried to settle myself and get warm.

Shafts of cold light came plunging down to illuminate the interior. The floor was strewn with huge fragments of broken rock from the ceiling and, here and there, the tracks of scorpions in the dust. I slept. At midnight I was wakened from a deep sleep by a tremendous scream that drilled clean through my head and literally made my hair stand on end.

"Who the hell is that?" I shouted out to the stone walls.

If it sounded again, I was going to make a four-hundred-mile dash for the coast and break my own record swimming back to Europe. But though I sat up for an hour, watching the moon set, not another sound came. As I drifted off again, I said to myself, "Those Berbers have a peculiar sense of humor."

Throughout the High Atlas I could not stop climbing, even though I could see that I was heading into impassable snowfields and masses of ice and broken rock, which called for climbing skills I did not have even with the aid of my crampons. The brilliance of the equatorial sun on all that snow was cold white fire at my feet. The wind froze like winter, and I shivered and sweated at the same time. Beyond the snow and rock lay the Sahara, and I was anxious now to reach it and be on my way to Agadir.

The passage through the mountains became a dream as I slogged along through patches of snow, with heavy mists running down out of black clouds and sudden, electrifying views of the desert appearing in slots through the clouds, like mythical kingdoms in the sky. Then one day, when I had wakened before dawn and was making tea over a tiny fire, I saw that the pass in which I was camped opened out slightly above me, and there, stretched out in an immense, ocherous slash of nothingness, lay the Sahara. I came down the High Atlas at a half-run, stumbling and sweating in my excitement at having reached the desert.

The winds of the Sahara made the strangest sounds. They were like music. They spoke to me, like the voices that spoke to Ulysses when all his crew members had their ears filled with wadding. Ulysses was tied to the mast, and only he heard the Sirens' voices, the sounds of the wind. When the traveler is alone and the destination is far, it may be that there are always the voices of Sirens.

I could feel the atmosphere of the desert storing up inside me like a steel coil. One night a sirocco windstorm struck my campsite with dust so fine that it stuck in my eyes and then glued them shut. I had this thought: "Can a man walk to Agadir blind?" I decided that it was possible.

I was developing a confidence and trust in this lonely place. At once my eyes came unstuck.

There was a beautiful full moon one night, and I saw a man in a burnoose bent almost double, trying to push against a wind that I could not feel, because I was sheltering behind a dune. It reminded me of an old movie I had once seen, in which no matter how the characters tried, they could not walk down a street against the wind.

I settled into a yoga position, back against the ruins of an old tree, and meditated on the rising moon. I focused on the journey that was occurring inside my head. It was the storyteller's journey. In it I did not feel the sharp rocks under my burning feet or the rasping hot air in the back of my throat. I concentrated on never having to arrive in Agadir, but instead trying to connect with the formless, invisible atmosphere of the desert itself.

I had walked twelve hours that day and I was really ready for sleep. As I slipped into my sleeping bag, I saw the moonlight marching up the side of an enormous dune a few hundred yards away. It looked like a slow, white tidal wave forming. I could almost taste the salt. I composed my thoughts to walk sixty miles the next day. Thinking, I was discovering, was energy. Thoughts were actions, almost solid things that moved around in these untrammeled spaces. In a short time I was both warm and relaxed, and I slept without dreams.

But in daylight the desert had precisely the opposite effect. It encouraged dreams. It was an empty space waiting for something, or someone, to flow into it.

On the next day when I wakened, the sun was just bursting above some peaks in the far distance. Its light came rushing down into a nearby ravine that had been cut out of the desert by long-gone rains. I placed my water bottle in the left side of my pack, shrugged on my djelabah, and put on my sandals. In thirty seconds from waking I was on the road.

David as T. E. Lawrence, in the High Atlas. DAVID SMITH.

Here was the simplicity of pure action. But as I recognized this, my possessions, simple as they were, seemed to gain in weight because of the emptiness all around and above me. I had never realized that an absence of something could be a presence. I resented having to carry my stuff. I wanted to be completely stripped down, carrying nothing.

And that damned radio! I wished I'd given it to Mustapha. By what kind of reasoning had I decided that I would need a radio in the Sahara? I'd never even used it. Instead I just worried about losing it, which was taking my attention from feeling the desert.

Sometimes I would come upon tracks that looked as though they had been made by animals. Occasionally there would be a primitive kind of road. Often there was nothing. I began to see why people panicked when the path petered out and the horizon offered no orientation points. I passed the skeleton of a four-wheel-drive vehicle buried in the sand. I remembered a group of Germans who had recently driven into the eastern Sahara, trying to reach an oasis in the Qattara Depression, and for the lack of twenty-five cents worth of electrical wire, they all died.

The Bedouin have a saying that the "traveler will be betrayed by that which he does not love." The meaning of the word *love* here struck me like a blow. This conception of love was different from mine. I attached the emotion to women. The Bedouin attached it to place. I could feel a connection between them and nature in general. Those hard people of the desert wastes—the Tuareg, the Bedouin, the Berber—were united in their survival by a common affection that lay within the wilderness of sand. I was feeling this unity with the environment only after having been so long alone, surrounded by sand and pebbles.

Within minutes of any dawn the desert was a furnace of blazing heat. The sun skyrocketed upward with the same speed that it came plummeting down at night to disappear into some dark slot in the sand. In the open desert most people could stand this kind of heat without shade or water for about four hours, but the Bedouin could go a whole day without protection. I budgeted about four hours walking before I needed shelter. I did not plan to be picked up by anybody. I had come across a stone signpost that read, "Timbuktu: 56 days." I knew I could walk to Timbuktu, and that was a good feeling.

The heat seemed to get worse every day. It was hard to find anywhere to shelter. It was like drowning in sun. I had begun wearing the brown hood of the djelabah over my head, peaked into a kind of slit so that I did not have to face the glare. In silhouette I could see that I looked like a Berber.

I began to understand about personal power. That is, I could feel myself expanding as if to fill a space outside myself. The desert did not interfere with me. It didn't even have a tree to get in the way of me expanding. I did not have to walk around anything. Instead I could just feel the flow of dunes, the rush of space into distance.

Out of nowhere came a young Berber. He was alone, wearing a beanie, his hair cut very close to his head. He had on a white robe with a brown burnoose, and a purse was slung over his shoulder. He came right up to me and indicated that I should take his picture. I got a bad feeling from him. He was a very strong, hard-looking fellow. I refused to take his picture and walked on. He started following me and then insisted that I take his picture. I took it. Then he said he wanted money.

This was the moment I had been warned about. I pulled out a durham coin and gave it to him, but it was immediately clear that he wanted all the money. Now the aggression was really in the air, thick and dangerous. Instead of responding fearfully and running away, or defensively by slugging him, I quickly took the coin away from him. He put his hand out, demanding all my money again, but this time with a kind of a lunge. As he came at me, I gave him back the coin and my walking stick, and at the same time I used the energy of his lunge to seize his arm and direct him down the road toward the next village.

Unlike my bullfight this wasn't a thought followed by an action. It was pure action, thoughtless and effortless. It felt so new and strange to me that I felt I hadn't really done it at all. It was as if I had become simply a channel for the man's energy. Either there had been no "I" at all, or the strongest "I" that could be imagined.

I could see the man's face saying, "What is this? I was trying to rob this idiot and now I'm walking with him. Am I crazy?"

We kept up a fast pace through the heat for three hours, and while I was waiting for him to drop, I totally forgot my thirst. He was gasping, and I thought I had him licked. Then we came to a village where two women were trying to lift a 150-pound sack. I tried to lift it but could barely get it to my shoulder. The Berber reached down, picked it up, and slung it over his shoulder. Then he broke into a slow trot again, gesturing for me to hurry up, to follow him. This was his village, and it was just after six o'clock. The sun was almost down. Instead of taking my money he had his wife serve me a cup of tea. He was a family man. Had he ever been a robber?

The encounter with the Berber caused the desert to expand in a new way. I felt a tingling expectation inside. It was not angry but almost aggressive. Then I realized it was a feeling of adequacy. I had not been uncertain about who I was when confronted by the danger that everybody had warned me about. No one gave me any orders out there; there were no regulations, policemen, rules, or worries about consequences outside myself. There had been two men meeting on primitive terms, when either could have killed the other without penalty. Instead we had drunk tea.

I remembered Nietzsche's dictum of there being a natural will to power in every person. The desert helped this to be realized.

I reached Taroudant, a very old desert town, on the dusk of that day, then cleaned up and got a shave from a barber. I had been traveling nineteen days by that time, and I decided that I would finish the journey to Agadir on the twentieth day by walking sixty miles without stopping and without water.

By now I was well into the rhythms of the desert, whose message was to leave everything behind. There had been times when I felt like shucking off my shoes and walking barefoot. Everything inside me that I did not want was being drawn out, absorbed into the sand. I could feel the magnetism and electricity of the earth. Once again I felt the presence of the source, for the first time on land. I could smell it, hear it, sense it in hundreds of ways. I imagined or felt the stimulus of distant tides, the phases of the moon, the sense of the winds, so that I wanted the journey to go on and on. I had flowed into the desert, and it was mine. It was like reading a good book and not wanting it to end.

I set out at four thirty in the morning. If I could make it within the day, I would complete the journey while Ramadan was still on. About five miles into the desert I was stopped dead by a pair of glowing red eyes in front of me and the sound of a ferocious growl. It was as though I were in one of those little amusement-park cars that whip you into dark places, with all kinds of gadgets trying to scare the hell out of you. The difference was that this journey wasn't going to be over in a few minutes. There was no calling a cab and no lights to turn on.

But wait a minute! I had an automatic electric flash on my camera. Hurriedly I set it up and flashed it. There was nothing there. I heard noises as though animals were nearby, on water. But there was no water around. I was in the middle of a desert. The noises seemed to come from about fifty feet away. It sounded like things were moving around me. Then some person brushed by me going the other way, toward the High Atlas. It wasn't hard enough to throw me off balance—just shoulders barely rubbing each other— but it was enough to scare the hell out of me. I prayed for the sun. I was cold, and my feet were hurting. But more than anything I wanted light.

I tried jogging for five minutes and then walking for five, then jogging for five again. Little pebbles and rocks kicked up into my cheap sneakers, and the soles disintegrated. The stones stuck into my bleeding feet. I got really irritated—the desert was supposed to be made of sand, but instead it was all these damned little bits of rock and stone. Where did all these rocks come from? After the dawn light grew, I tried jumping between the rocks, trying to find places without sharp bits that would stick into my feet. Gradually the pain came upward from my bleeding soles, and then my knees hurt, and then my waist. I laughed at the thought that the upper part of my body did not hurt at all.

I arrived in Agadir at day's end, three hundred miles and twenty days of hiking behind me. I trudged in to the city that had been almost completely destroyed a few years before but that now looked brand new again, brilliantly white and clean.

I knew I would not have to ask for help. I met a really sweet men named Mohammed Douda, and we chatted about the city and about the great earthquake. Then he said, "You must come and celebrate the feast marking the end of Ramadan in my house." It sounded good to me.

I checked into a fancy hotel, the Mahabra, even though I was told initially that it was *complet*—full. I could understand why the Frenchman behind the polished reception desk might be skeptical of the filthy-looking, dust-clogged, thinned-down desert rat before him. I remembered that when Lawrence of Arabia came out of the desert one time and went to the officers' bar with an Arab boy, no one would serve him. I decided that if I looked like Lawrence of Arabia, I would start acting like him.

I raised hell. I shouted at the manager for a while, charging him with arrogance, discrimination, and everything else I could think of. But he was unmoved. So I tried another tack.

"Look," I said, "I've been up there in the Atlas mountains, and when I got to the top, I could see the desert on one side and the Mediterranean on the other. It was this great contrast."

He looked absolutely blank.

"Now," I said, "I've been in the desert, and I want another great contrast."

"Monsieur?"

"One of your beautiful, comfortable rooms."

He grinned. He could understand that. In a minute I was in one of the hotel's best suites.

I took off my clothes and jumped into a bath; then I showered. I cleaned myself like I would an expensive automobile. When I dried off and looked in the mirror, I saw my entire body for the first time in three weeks.

Who on earth was this?

I hadn't thought about losing weight during Ramadan. In Marrakech, Mustapha had said, "Ramadan cleans you out." But now I had an entirely different body. I was standing there in front of a stranger—a lean, hard-looking fellow, like that Berber in the desert. Then I really freaked out. I thought, "What do I do with this body?"

Suddenly I began to cry. I had gone through a complete metamorphosis. It had been a radical change from my water world to sand, and a swimmer lay dead in the desert. More panic. Damn, my old body had been a good one! What if this one didn't work as well?

Then, as suddenly as I had begun crying, I started to laugh. I realized that I had gone through an immense physical challenge with this new body; so it must be a good one. My emotion had more to do with the mental change I'd undergone than the physical one. I relaxed a little. At this point the entire trip came flashing back through my mind, and I just felt elated, cleansed and new.

A few days later I had a wonderful time with Mohammed Douda and his family, celebrating the end of Ramadan in style. I told them many stories about my desert trek. We laughed nearly as much as we talked. I could feel the change that had come upon me in the desert. I had left behind what I did not want, what I did not need to carry anymore.

I said to my hosts, "You know, there's something very strange out there in the desert. It's like a force that works to help you. In fact, it's like some kind of medicine."

To my surprise, Mohammed Douda knew what I was talking about.

"Of course the desert heals," he said, smiling. "Everybody knows that."

Chapter 4

Pioneer

The head-shaven black man who stepped up onto the starting podium of the Olympic-sized swimming pool in Brooklyn Heights looked like an advertisement for raw muscle power. His biceps bulged like melons. The hard lines of three stacks of muscles across his belly showed that drug abuse had not yet ruined his physique. He was a convicted felon for burglary, mugging, assault, and a few lesser charges. But to me his body spoke most eloquently about his life. It told me what he could be rather than what he had been. And I, unlike the law, was much more interested in the athlete than in the drug addict.

The man's name was Tiger Robinson, and he paused there and looked straight at me, dark eyes brooding with the history of his life.

"All right, you white motherfucker," he said. "You ain't never goin' to teach me to swim."

With that he leaped into the water and sank like a stone. I waited a beat before diving in to save him. He was the tenth guy I had saved that month.

For two years after my walk across the High Atlas and the Sahara, I ranged the world, seeking out new opportunities to demonstrate the source phenomenon to myself and to others. The Moroccan walk had shown me that I did not need to swim in order to tap the source, and the world seemed spread out like a feast awaiting my arrival. I became a lecturer at health conferences. I wrote magazine articles and appeared on television talk shows. I even served as a fitness consultant at a meeting of physicists interested in psychic research, at Reykjavik, Iceland.

I put together a series of one-man sporting events that pitted me against a place or a problem or myself. One of these was a cluster of "happenings" in North Africa that I called the Everyman's Olympics. These were in part a good-humored protest against the nationalistic competitiveness of the Olympics, which reached its zenith at the 1972 Games in Munich. The assassination of Israeli athletes by Palestinian terrorists took away the humor but sharpened the point I was making.

In the Caribbean I staged the Peace Pentathlon, a group of events that expressed the joy of competing with oneself. One event was a marathon run in Haiti designed to create a bridge of understanding between blacks and whites. I ran through a busy market village, the roads packed with vendors and buyers, all the way to Papa Doc Duvalier's palace on the other side of the mountains, where I delivered a message of brotherhood at the palace gates.

It was impossible to experience the surging energies of the source without being impelled to share them. I could not describe my feelings, but I could act them out. People understood that. Also, after spending some time in the Orient I had become aware of a tradition in which the source had spiritual relevance. The Eastern peoples, I found, understood what I was getting at even if they had different ways of expressing it.

The Japanese believed that energy flowed from the earth, but that it had to be controlled, almost quelled, by self-discipline and restraint. I studied the martial arts in Tokyo and Hong Kong and found that "less is more," as the Zen teachers emphasized. Achievement should be effortless, they said repeatedly.

In Delhi I worked at a yoga hospital, getting firsthand experience in both the theory and practice of releasing the body's energies to cure itself. I spent time in an ashram in the Himalayas, where I discovered that without saying a word the Yogis were obeying exactly the same rules of yielding to the flow of energy as were the kendo experts and the medics of the Delhi hospital.

In all of this Eastern experience I found no trace of the urgent competitiveness that made us all so tense in the West. When I returned to New York, I was ready for a project that would put me directly in touch with some of the things that were most troublesome in my own country.

When I reached New York, my friend David Brink called to ask whether I wanted to become a physical fitness consultant to a program designed to rehabilitate drug addicts. David directed the "Pioneer Program" for the South Street Seaport Museum; the objective of the Pioneer Marine School was to train qualified service people for the marine industry up and down the eastern coast of the United States.

Nobody knows how many drug addicts there are in New York. Counting all the people who cannot get through a day without some form of drug support—which may range from swallowing a handful of amphetamines to shooting up near-lethal doses of heroin—the number may run into the millions.

Tiger Robinson was a mainliner. Twenty years ago his case would have been considered hopeless, but now it was dawning on society that the drug addict, like the alcoholic, destroyed himself for a reason. If the reason could be found and rectified, or some other motivating power put into the addict's life, then he could be turned around. The problem could be seen as a matter of displaced energy, of the person's being totally cut off from the source. Addicts were people who had become disconnected from the roots of their being.

But Brink found himself in trouble almost as soon as the program started. He discovered that his trainees were falling asleep at their desks by nine in the morning. They were in poor physical shape. Their diet was heavy on doughnuts and coffee. They had no energy, and, most ironically, few of them could swim, even though they were being trained for work that would put them on or near the water most of their working day.

"Can you teach them to swim, first," asked Brink, "and then wake them up, second? Well, wait a minute! Maybe we should reverse that. Wake them up first, then teach them to swim."

"If they learn to swim, they'll be awake," I said, accepting the challenge.

After I fished Tiger out of the water, to his contempt and anger—"If I'd a drowned, honky, you'd a lost your job, heh?"—I understood that I was dealing with a man who fundamentally was in a state of barely suppressed fury all the time.

The drug addict is a man against himself. He does not run with his muscles. He is in flight in his mind, racing his ruined body toward destruction rather the conservation. When I swam in the pool, I got to the other end. Tiger sank to the bottom. We both achieved our objectives, but his were hate-filled. He got what he wanted by depriving somebody else of what they wanted.

One of Tiger's problems was physiological. He had been a superb physical specimen who before his addiction had worked out with weights. Through his addiction he had turned against his body, punishing it with drugs rather than rewarding it with exercise. Like any finely tuned and highly developed machine, Tiger's body begged to be used to its full capabilities. Anything less was a negation of identity and purpose.

But Tiger's energy had to go somewhere, and he had found no other outlet than to turn it back on himself. The adrenaline flow that he might have gotten from projecting his life to success, satisfaction, and achievement of well-being could be stimulated only through negative activity—

Pioneer participants during exercise session. DAVID SMITH.

putting people down, shooting himself up, and, now, fighting me for sway over himself and the other men. I could guess that the entire hormonal balance of his body was in disarray.

Ron Lawrence, a former surgeon who developed a specialized practice of treating pain, often through acupuncture, told me once that when the body cannot manufacture the drugs—hormones—that it needs, it will give instructions for them to be procured. A craving develops. The catch may be that the body's "drugs," which include such exotic substances as the neurotransmitters dopamine, serotonin, and norepinephrine, are not procurable over the counter or from drug pushers. In seeking substitutes the body's drive is to change behavior in search of the right stuff. Hence negative and destructive behavior, including, for some, drug addiction, as a means of getting at least short-term relief from the overall chemical and mental anarchy of the victim.

Part of my function in the Pioneer Program was to stimulate the production of natural drugs through discipline and exercise, and hope that some of it would catch hold.

Tiger was angry, and that was good. The defense against anger was apathy, and in apathy lay the imperilment of the program. I was dealing with demons here, both quiescent and aroused, and it was these demons that I needed to harness to get the addicts to work.

"Don't kid yourself, buddy," I had told Tiger. "They'll send you back to the slammer before they fire me."

He just glowered.

Tiger Robinson's technique of dealing with this new "problem" in his life—yet another effort by society to reform him—was revealed in the early days of the program. He sought to move into my territory and make it his own, or at least use it as a base for restructuring his own attack on life. Aggression, I knew, was a fundamental statement of identity or self-assertion. But a big, dangerous-looking black man does not get the nod from society when he threatens to smash it. His hatred prevents him from making that vital statement "I am" without society insisting that he is wrongheaded, antisocial, and criminal.

Tiger was raw power. Everything he did was expressed in terms of force, even to the threat of drowning as a means of avoiding learning to swim. Whatever I was for, he was against. He blew cigarette smoke in my face. He ground his heels onto my toes. He threatened the first fellow addict in my class who showed signs of becoming competent in the water.

Tiger achieved his identity, or his potency, by suppressing or smothering the drive in others as well as himself. When I swam demonstration laps, which held the class's attention, he was enraged, because it cut down his power, his identity.

"I doubt you'll do much with Tiger," one of the Pioneer staffers warned me. "Just try and prevent him from infecting the other men."

David Brink was a bit more optimistic: "See if you can break through to him without getting yourself killed." Tiger had all the talents for his own salvation. I decided to make him a leader.

"I don't need to teach you how to swim," I said. "You're a natural athlete, and you could pick it up in a few minutes. So I'm gonna get you to teach the others."

"You out of your ever-lovin' mind? I wouldn't help you if you paid for it, honky pig!"

I never paid any attention to his outbursts but instead just assumed that he wanted to help me. I told him there were two men in the class—Raimondo and Pepe—who needed help.

"Go eat shit!"

One day I dived into the deep end and peeled off a superfast 100 meters. All at once the whole class, except Tiger, began hurling themselves into the water, swimmers or not. As I swam, I saw Tiger leave for the dressing rooms, but at least he looked back once. Though he was leaving the group, he did not quite want to now.

Early on, Peter Sanford, president of the South Street Seaport Museum, talked to the group, giving them background on the program. "You're part of the history of concern," he said. "Nobody's really alone if they have some faith in the world. We're trying to put new purposes into old roots. The city has to provide new horizons. We're proud of what's happening here at the museum."

The response of my wise-cracking addicts was simple and direct.

"Wha?"

Captain Geo Matteson, skipper of the schooner *Pioneer,* the South Street vessel on which we would eventually sail, came into a swimming session and talked about the trip we were going to take. That got the group's attention. A sail? You mean, on the sea, man? Hey, that's cool-ass! I get to steer it first!

Matteson said, "A sailing vessel is a unique environment in which responsibility, companionship, and self-knowledge may be fostered."

"Wha?"

He described the difficulties of operating a large sailing ship. It would be cramped. There would have to be teamwork, cooperation.

"Wha?"

The Addiction Services Agency and its drug-free day care centers and community live-in centers would be vitally interested in the results.

Yawns all around.

My friend Ron Lawrence believes that if you want to communicate about one thing, you talk about another thing. "It's called lateral thinking," he says. "Sneaking up on the problem from an unexpected direction. Making use of the random energy of the universe. It'll take you along in ways you could never have predicted."

That's what I needed to reach these addicts. Telling them what was good for them provoked only boredom. Metaphor was needed, in the Lawrence manner, if I wanted to get them to deal with their dilemma.

So before we swam every day, we talked. The addicts were suspicious at first and said little about their lives. There was not much to tell—there was really just one story. I remembered the old storyteller in Marrakech whose sole worldly possessions were a mat, some old copper, a few bowls, and a lamp. But he was better off, in his head, anyway, than these urban misfits. They all came from broken families. The parents had been overwhelmed by responsibilities, and one or both had split. The community was faceless, the days a grinding routine of trying to make ends meet and dodging the cops. The only real game in town was run by the drug people. There adrenaline flowed. It was a shot against hopelessness and failure.

"I only know one thing," said Raimondo. "That life's a crock."

I got them into stories.

"You know about the Olympic Games?"

Guarded nods.

"I was in this plane, over the ocean, and getting ready to parachute."

"You jumpin' into the sea with a parachute? You some kinda crazy man?"

"I was in a kind of race, through the air, the water, across the sand, up the mountain, to find a gorgeous girl, who would reward me for my efforts."

"Yeah, man!"

"And then a magazine, *Sports Illustrated*, wrote up the whole thing as a story."

"I don't get it," said Raimondo.

"The cat was swimmin' and jumpin' and tearin' up the mountain instead of wastin' himself, you junkie," said Pepe.

"You get chicks, with all this clean-livin' shit?"

The dialogue was begun.

We swapped stories in the pool, as I taught them to float, kick, and stroke. Dick Rath, chairman of the Pioneer Committee, came down to the hotel where the pool was located to talk to us.

"You're going to enjoy the sailing part," he said. The idea that this scruffy, desperate-looking gang would go to sea in anything except a heavily guarded prison ship almost made me break up. "The *Pioneer* is a historic vessel, and you'll feel her history."

What these guys actually felt was a twenty-four-hour-a-day longing for a needle in the arm and release from this "bummer feeling" they had most of the time.

"She was built in 1885, and she was just a utility vessel in those days. She's worked hard all through her life, as a freighter, as a harbor tanker, and later as a self-powered construction barge."

"She ever bin in the slammer?" asked Tiger, guffawing.

"Then Russ Grinnel rebuilt her in 1968, and she went right back to work, hauling piles and equipment for waterfront construction. Today she's doing the most interesting work of all, teaching ex-addicts something about the responsibilities and rewards of the sea."

"It's a crock of shit with sails," said Raimondo.

Physical exertion siphoned off some of the negative energy. The longer they swam this day, the longer they could swim the next day, and I arranged it so that swimming time could be made to cut into class time, to give them incentive for one good thing at the expense of another good thing. But the important thing was the ability to communicate incentive at all. If they could swim out of class, they might be able to swim out of their habits.

They began to tell stories and looked forward to hearing them.

"Hit us with a story," they would chorus.

"I was locked up, all night, in a cave in Gibraltar," I said.

"Why'd you do a thing like that, man?"

"It was part of the Everyman's Olympics. I wanted to see if I was frightened of anything. I carried some silk thread with me so I could find my way back. Then, at midnight, I heard this weird cry. . . ."

"It was your old lady lookin' for you."

My stories were part of the exercise plan. They laid down tracks in the consciousness, roadways to the men's minds in which an environment was created and filled with symbols disguised as actions—the outdoors, action adventures, stories about me as a figure they could identify with, the hero runner at work.

The smoldering Tiger remained out of most of our discussions. But he was swimming and improving. He would slip into the water and push himself off with a short kick of his powerful legs. He went underwater each time—his way of saying that he did not want to be watched—before coming up again, surprisingly, about halfway down the pool. Then he swam with short, chopping strokes, raising lots of angry foam but pushing himself along.

I tried to work the men to near-exhaustion, but that was almost impossible. They had no basis for understanding physical exertion as anything but either punishment or exploitation by somebody else. Feeling good to them was being on junk. But the water had a cleansing effect. It was also a tranquilizer, massaging as well as supporting. Enjoyment started to grow. They were becoming hooked.

But, of course, I could not take them beyond these tiled walls, these echoing rooms with lockers and benches that evoked prison more than freedom from junk. Ideally I wanted the men out in the woods or the desert. After three weeks I started using post-workout talk sessions as well as our preswim talks. These usually took place in the locker room, as

I went over what they had learned and what to watch for in the future, and it was during one of these sessions that Tiger, who had remained sullenly silent as his swimming improved, suddenly became animated.

"More of them stories," he demanded. "Now!"

"You want stories about swimming?"

"I want stories about *thinkin'* about the swimmin'," he growled.

"You got it!" I cried. "Thinking about it! Anybody here know what that's called?"

A blank, but flickering interest.

"Meditation," I said.

"What's that shit?" they asked, suspiciously taking in the new word.

"It's like concentrating," I said. "It's pouring everything you've got in your head into one place so that you can break through to a new place."

"Like developin' a good kick," ventured Raimondo.

"You got it! It's freeing the mind from many objects of distraction and fixing attention on one point. It's an extension of concentration, actually, where you're tuned into something other than your own mind and thought chatter, all that shit inside you that runs around in the head like a rabbit, going nowhere. Doing it, you're going to make both your mind and your body calm."

There was a strange stillness. Something had gotten to them.

"Meditation," one of them said, trying it out.

"A crock," said Tiger, but without real conviction.

"Here I am, closing my eyes," I said, closing my eyes, "and I'm working on it, just as hard as if I'm swimming. I'm in the dark, but bringing that last bit of light in the locker room to a point just above my eyebrows. That's what I do. You can do any damn thing you like. My thoughts are taking me away. I'm flying."

I was flying.

"See, I'm breathing from my diaphragm," I said, eyes still closed, "from this place just under the ribs. I feel secure and serene. I feel the water all around me, and I'm racing through a thousand meters. I'm floating through beautiful farmland. The birds are singing, and there's a pond with frogs croaking in it."

"He's flipped his turtle."

I opened my eyes suddenly.

"I have a story," I said.

"Anything would be better than this meddertoshin shit," said Tiger.

"I'll tell you a story about meditation," I said. "I took a trip around the world about a year ago. I persuaded Air France to give me a round-the-world ticket if I mentioned their airline in one of my magazine stories."

"No shit!"

This was heavy stuff, getting it for free. My stock went up eleven thousand percent.

"When I was in Tokyo, in Japan, a woman in my hotel told me there was a shrine to soldiers of World War II in back of the hotel, where I could meditate. I checked it out, and it looked like a really good place to get some peace and quiet. It looked marvelously cool and peaceful, an ideal spot to sit and just let the thoughts flow. I rang the doorbell of a huge mansion in front of the meditation garden, but there was no answer. Probably too early, I figured. So I walked around the house and found a door to the garden that was half open. I went in and sat in front of a pond near two pillars.

"I got into it very quickly. A car honking took my mind to Japanese taxis and the little lever that the drivers use to open the doors, and this took me to automation, and all those little people bent over machines, putting them together, and so to pollution, and streets with no numbers along them, and everybody being lost, and I thought of the ocean I had flown over, and the oneness of water, and then there was a wave, and I became a wave, and I was just flowing, flowing, flowing, in constant change, yet remaining myself. "Then I heard a voice in the distance. 'Can I help?' it was saying, and then it came again. 'Can I do anything for you?'

"The voice seemed kind of harsh, and I looked up and saw two Japanese men standing there, looking rather ruffled. I shook my head and looked back toward the beautiful garden.

"But they didn't go away. One of them demanded, 'What do you want?' I looked at him. 'I want the peace and quiet of this garden,' I said. I was thinking, 'Boy, these Japanese fellows have some strange attitude about their memorial meditation garden for war heroes.'

"But my response just seemed to make the man angrier. He really got worked up. 'Do you know where you are?' he shouted in my ear. With great dignity I said, 'I am in the shrine to World War II soldiers, and I wish you would bug out of here.'

"He shouted back at me, 'You are in the private residence of the ambassador from the Philippines!' "

"You were in this cat's house," said Pepe.

"You was in a burglarizin' position," said another.

There was a general breakup as they whacked each other's shoulders and fell down laughing, hooting, pounding the floor and slapping palms.

"That was no meddertashun. It was the cat's garden!"

They couldn't get over it. For the rest of our time together it was the standing joke.

The program really began to come together in the fourth week. I had calculated each man's physical limits and then pushed him along for another few laps. Some did it; others could not. I thought if I could tire them out, then I could work on them afterward. But their minds were so filled with the negative junk from their past that breaking through it was a major task.

The greater the stress they suffered, in effort and through my own exhortations, the more energy they had the next day. It might have looked like magic to an outsider, but they were simply riding low-level highs that any athlete gets by focusing his energies. Even Tiger, who had begun swimming with me, started to develop some pride in his stroke, which was really not much more than a dog-paddle yet.

We worked out day after day. In two months they could all swim, in a fashion.

"Hey," shouted Pepe, coming to the surface, the water streaming from his straggly beard, "you tell me I never sweem, eh? Look here, a feesh! I sweem like a feesh!"

After each session I got them all out of the water and sitting on the tiles with their eyes closed while I encouraged them to think outside themselves.

"Think 'green fields,' " I said in a soft voice.

They replied in unison, "Green fields!"

"Think 'blue skies,' " I directed.

They shouted, "blue skies!"

"Think 'I dig green fields.'"

"We dig green fields!"

"Think 'I dig blue skies.' "

"We dig blue skies!"

By the time we were ready for the *Pioneer* sail they made almost daily jokes about this mindless routine, which, I hoped, was taking them at least vicariously out of these artificial, stultifying surroundings and liberating their imaginations into places where they might be free.

One of my big problems was to get them relaxed. I got them into contraction-relaxation exercises, systematically working on all parts of the body while they breathed diaphragmatically.

"Imagine you're going down in an elevator," I said, "lower and lower. Now you're on an escalator, going down, down, down. While you're doing that, count from ten to one. Then get off the escalator. Now go to this place, this safe and beautiful place, and relax."

I told them that my favorite safe and beautiful place was on Mount Tamalpais in Marin County, north of San Francisco, overlooking the Pacific Ocean. It was on the slope of the mountain, with trees everywhere and a terrific wide view of the Pacific.

"Now stay in your place, breathing deeply into your belly, for fifteen minutes."

Then I would slowly bring them out of their places.

The essence of the journey to the source is the recognition that the traveler is alone, yet is joined to everything else. The group dynamic emphasizes the feeling of connectedness, but it also fosters a dependency on group action and a greater difficulty, it seems to me, in acquiring the individual identity that leads to recovery. Energy flows more easily in a group, and it fools everybody into thinking they're making better progress than they really are.

But the change in the group was remarkable. When we mounted the gangplank of the *Pioneer* at Newport, Rhode Island, there was a lot of kidding around about hijacking the schooner and taking it to the Caribbean for a real holiday. It was a gorgeous day, with brilliant blue skies and winds as soft as butter. Tiny, white-capped waves broke in flashes of foam from energy given them by the stiff wind that had blown up the previous night.

It was time to move beyond the "abandonment" of the old identity to the threshold the men needed to view a possible new life. There they would be different people. But what was identity to them? Emphasizing the positive usually had been a trick that society used to get them to do what they did not want to do. The people with the greatest control over them, I had learned in our numerous bull sessions, had little success in helping the addicts reconstruct a sense of themselves. These were people in the "regulatory industries," as I described them—social workers, police, penal system officials—who knew a lot about regulation but practically nothing about addiction. Some were on power trips, people who got their kicks from demanding obedience to orders and rules that had little or nothing to do with the condition of the man suffering the regulation. The addicts' journey was a search for the part of self that was being suppressed by almost every act of the society in which they lived. "Blue skies!" shouted Raimondo as we went aboard, and everybody except the people already on the *Pioneer* understood what he meant. It was my hope that the men's hidden, paralyzing rage at themselves would melt away in the near-total freedom of being at sea and so much further removed from day-to-day influences.

In the past few months the men had stopped killing themselves with drugs, and they were not ripping off society anymore. They had a new sense of achievement in their bodies. Their classwork was going moderately well. Could they complete their quest for identity under the *Pioneer*'s sails and finish their healing journey at sea?

I had been watching Tiger as my model. He was the angriest, strongest, toughest, and smartest—and the worst criminal. The greater the crime, the stronger the energy of the criminal. Energy to overcome, energy to keep going down the long marathon haul of the wilderness they were going into. Tiger had the best chance to connect with the source. But he was also the most likely to put up drastic and desperate resistance to such a fate.

As we sailed into the sound, the schooner heeling in the strong breeze, I felt my body coming alive. Tiger was watching me. The captain, Geo Matteson, told me that Tiger and I had the nine-to-eleven evening watch. As we got ourselves settled, there were delicious butterscotch brownies to eat, and the orange-pink moon soon turned a whitish yellow. I saw Tiger at the rail by himself, and I joined him. About an hour passed.

"People git paid to sail these things?" he asked finally.

"Sure," I said.

"I mean, would it be steady workin'?" he went on, trying not to make it a question at all.

"Sure," I said.

"It's the dumbest thing I ever saw," he said, "usin' wind when you could go engine." And he went below.

Tiger didn't show up for our watch, but at dawn, when I was up on deck meditating through the sunrise, he turned up. We were coming into a beautiful cove, and I could see a seventeenth-century house and barn overlooking the horseshoe-shaped, tree-lined beach. Six other boats were anchored in the tiny cove.

"You wanna swim ashore and take a run?" Tiger was at my elbow.

We dived in together and headed for the shore. The early morning light was silvery with silklike clouds behind the green trees. The tan-brown beach was free of debris. We started running and felt pebbles under our feet. A small lake was tucked into the trees near the beach. There wasn't a person in sight. The *Pioneer* looked like a pirate ship when I looked at it through my fingers to isolate it from the other boats.

We must have run about two miles. When we got back to the beach, we could see figures on deck. I knew we both had a feeling of having shared something that was ours alone, and that Tiger liked it. We plunged into the water, and when we hauled up onto the deck where the others were eating a pancake breakfast, Tiger walked slowly down the waist of the ship and said to the others, "You monkeys missed the sun comin' up beside the old house under the oak trees."

Nobody had the faintest idea what he was talking about.

I had never thought about a quest for identity until I found my own changed by exposure to the source. But observing the Pioneer men in their fortresses of insecurity, I understood that the quest could be a life-or-death journey. The affirmation of the self, once identity has become a pos-

The cutter Eagle *races* Pioneer, *near Newport.* DAVID SMITH.

sibility, could release great reserves of pent-up energy as the life-support systems are hooked up to the big power pack beneath. Here we were, I felt, ready for that empowering jolt. The men had succeeded in acquiring swimming skills and a lot of knowledge about repairing marine engines, and now they were free from society's dictates, on a sailing ship, gliding through calm waters. I figured it was something very close to paradise.

Instead there was something terribly wrong.

I could not describe it right away because, forgetting Ron Lawrence, I was not thinking laterally. Nobody was, and that was the problem. Tiger and his group were almost free of the overbearing society that had contributed to their rage. But they were also free of our swimming disciplines, our training routines, the direction and scope of our self-indoctrination to recovery. Our group discipline could not be replaced yet by the most onerous of all disciplines, that of the self. On the *Pioneer*, that was the men's plight and our mutual failure.

But the problem went even deeper. It had something to do with traveling first class. This was the trip of a lifetime; there was nothing to fight against, no stress. Of course, I had to remind myself yet again, it was stress that led me to the source and kept me within its embrace. It was stress that mobilized the body's forces and animated the mind. Stress had to be present in the environment in the right way, to enable the body to release the right chemicals for right action. The luxury of the *Pioneer* sail, although novel, did not relate to any kind of new life the men could believe in and strive for.

They fell apart. They drew into themselves as we spanked into those glorious, fresh ocean winds, and the sun poured down, and we rolled and creaked in the grip of the swells. They were sacked out in their bunks or on deck snoring in the scuppers, bored out of their skulls. In planning their "escape" from society, nobody had considered the possibility that in paradise there might be nothing to do.

We sailed to Martha's Vineyard, Nantucket, and Block Island, but these places might as well have been on the moon. When we sailed into Mystic Seaport, one of the guys was sick with "too much fresh food." It took a large order of french fries to set him straight. I had lost my persuasion with the men. I was no longer the swimming instructor but just another crewman. The undemanding environment was strange to me, too.

We sailed under the Newport bridge as we headed for home, and I helped change the jib when the schooner went hard to the lee to come around. Apathy lay on the *Pioneer*. I made my usual announcement that anybody who wanted to join me in yoga could come amidships in a few minutes. The men wanted to learn, I knew that. But the ship was out of their control. What a pity we didn't have a sail-raising every few minutes. It would pull the guys together.

Sail-raising on Pioneer. DAVID SMITH.

We passed under another bridge and, in a while, Geo dropped the anchor. We started taking down the sails. I was standing near the halyard that controls the dropping of the peak of the foresail gaff. I asked the second mate, Skip Grinnel, whose father had bought and rebuilt the *Pioneer* five years earlier, if I could help at this position. Several men already held the rope, but Tiger joined them.

Skip said, "It only needs one man to tend it." I jumped over to help furl the sail as it stacked up on top of the boom.

The gaff was almost at its lowest point when all the men on the halyard except Tiger let go. The halyard slipped around the pin as Tiger, caught off guard by the full weight of the gaff, struggled to prevent it from slipping through his fingers. He almost succeeded, but the gaff dropped on Geo's head. As Geo sank to his knees, blood streaming from his head, it was hard to say whether he or Tiger had the more stunned expression on his face. Tiger's eyes became as big as pool balls. He wasn't sullen or angry, not himself at all. He just looked as though he had made a very frightening backward journey to a place that he had been desperately trying to forget.

We all crowded around Geo, who was unconscious and looked really bad; so it was a big surprise when Raimondo suddenly cried out, "Tiger's making a run for it!"

I rushed to the rail with some of the others. Tiger was swimming fast, a real crawl stroke, toward the shore.

"Hey, sucker!" shouted Pepe. "They gonna shoot you, soon as you hit the shore!"

But our attention soon swung back to Geo, who was coming to consciousness, groaning and bleeding. Guys were rushing around getting water and bandages and ice cubes, and Geo was saying he was okay, not to worry, everything was going to be fine. Before long I heard a siren in the distance, and when I looked ashore, an ambulance was pulling up at the wharf. Standing on the wharf was Tiger, waving.

We got Geo ashore in one of our rowboats, and he was in the hospital in about fifteen minutes. Geo thanked Tiger for thinking so fast and acting so quickly.

The Pioneer Program was pretty successful, I heard. There were more than 1000 graduates in eight years, with a job placement rate of over 65% of incoming students. A few of them went back on junk, though, and one was killed in a hold-up attempt in Brooklyn. Tiger Robinson landed a job repairing outboard engines in Portsmouth, New Hampshire. But he was a very active, restless man, his employer said, and he left for California after a year. As far as I know, he never appeared in the public records again.

Chapter 5

Kayak from Khartoum

At the point where it reaches Khartoum, the White Nile is already two thousand miles from its origins in Lake Victoria, in the Tanzania-Kenya-Uganda conjunction. But it is the small and swifter Blue Nile that gives drama and color and force to the rivers' meeting. That was why we had chosen to start on it, and be swept down to its collision with the White Nile about three miles downriver from our starting point of Khartoum, in Sudan.

The Blue Nile—which is actually blue only very early in the morning—moves visibly quickly toward its meeting with the White Nile. In its rushing passage from the highlands of Ethiopia, it annually brings down millions of tons of silt, grit, and clay that eventually will be dumped in Egypt, much of it now laid down along the base of the Aswan High Dam. At its most powerful, in December and January, the Blue Nile actually dams up the White Nile and holds it in a kind of bondage until its force abates and the two rivers can flow together freely again. From Khartoum northward the Nile runs almost wholly within desert banks, or through land so parched that only meager subsistence farming is possible anywhere that has not been irrigated.

Six months earlier, in New York City, I had met an engaging Tunisian named Cherif Zaouch. He had invited me to visit him in Tunisia and ride horses with him over the desert from there to Morocco. Since I'd made one desert journey already and had yet to try a lengthy river trip, I made a counter-offer. Would he join me, instead, in a kayak trip down the Nile? He accepted, and the trip was on.

For me, the most powerful aspect of the Nile was its seeming changelessness. In modern times the great river has been civilized and controlled, chiefly by the mammoth dam at Aswan, yet throughout our journey I was struck by its quality of wildness almost untouched by the five thousand years of history lining its banks. The Emperor Nero's centurions came up the Nile, trying to find its source and, incidentally, the origin of Africa's gold. Herodotus traveled the river in search of strange and compelling stories for his histories. Many of its voyagers, both ancient and modern, have spoken feelingly of the mighty river's impact on mind and body, have made it a symbol of the flow of all life. As Alan Moorehead wrote in *The White Nile*, "It is a never-ending flood of warm, life-giving water that spans half of Africa from the Equator to the Mediterranean, and it is still the mightiest river on the earth."

A magazine assignment to report on the trip helped pay the costs. I didn't think I needed to learn kayaking skills, since there would be two thousand miles of on-the-job training. As we loaded our gear into the big, sturdy folding kayaks and pushed ourselves out onto the Blue Nile at Khartoum, a group of fascinated Sudanese, who had been watching our every move from shore, waved us good-bye. Most of them, we discovered, had no idea where the river went. Some of them had never even heard of the Mediterranean. At once, afloat and rocking gently in the swirl of the water, I could feel the insistence of the river's flow, gentle but irresistible. I felt the energy coming uninter-

A curious crowd attends the embarkation, near Khartoum.
DAVID SMITH.

ruptedly from its distant source and understood how this
fluid power could hold another river in check by the con-
tinuity of its force.

Khartoum passed by in a slow slide of dun-colored earth
and profuse palms over the variegated square buildings. In
an hour, as the Blue Nile began its turn north toward Egypt,
we glimpsed the White Nile ahead to our left. By keeping
up our steady paddling we placed ourselves along the line
of the confluence of the two rivers. The waters did not unite
easily. The White Nile was a kind of muddy gray around
my left paddle blade; the Blue Nile was greenish on my
right. I felt the split of energies, the vast differences in their
sources.

As the sun began to set that first day, we paddled over
to a sand dune island and set up our dome-shaped tent. We
knew nothing about the Nubians living along the river here
and were not yet ready to risk camping on the mainland.

When we had everything set up, the arched doorway of the tent framed a mosque across the river. I zipped down the back window and immediately saw a pirogue, a kind of roughly built Nile fishing boat, bearing down on the island.

"Uh-oh," I said to Cherif. "We've got visitors."

I had been too long in civilized environments, with their fears and prejudices, to be clear in the mind here. We were eating bread, honey, and olive oil when the boat ground to a halt on the beach in front of us. In it were a couple of tough-looking fellows who had tracked us from Khartoum. We continued to eat but tensed up a bit as they approached.

The men jumped onto the beach.

"You drop this," they said.

It was one of our smaller packs, which Cherif had left on the bank at the start.

After our visitors had dined with us—on hard-boiled eggs, olive oil, onions, garlic, bread sticks, oranges, and a handful of almonds—and left for Khartoum, we hugged each other happily.

"These Nubians are honest people," I said.

"That is why the Babylonians made such good slaves out of them," Cherif replied.

Our next days on the Nile were a fusion of time. The river was slow. Sometimes wind from the north drove us backward against the current. There was no feeling of going north at all. As we struggled to make progress in this vast expanse of water, Cherif was moved to comment upon the unexpected lack of push from the river's strong current. "This can't be a river," he said. "It's a gigantic lake!"

One by one our connections with the outside world dropped away, and our sense of place and time eroded. But not without a struggle, and not without accompanying stress.

The stress of being on the river was more than physical. There was stress generated by the attendant unknowns of our journey—lingering anxieties concerning the people we would encounter along the way, the crocodiles that might pose a danger to us on the river. Most of all the threat of bilharzia was a haunting presence. This horrible disease, carried by a microscopic leech, can debilitate a person for life, and there is no simple cure for it. The only measure of prevention we could take was to keep the Nile waters—in which the disease is carried—off ourselves as much as possible.

The physical stress of the trip was ultimately a catalyst for change. At the start of our journey I had noticed Cherif's flabby triceps. In twenty-five days his body had been transformed; it was lean, brown, and toughened. My shoulder muscles started to bulge. We were up with the sun each morning, then thirty minutes of yoga followed by a short run. Breakfast consisted of Sudanese flat bread, tahini, and honey. We paddled ten hours on some days. The river began to flow like wine.

Near Shendi we saw two men working with a net stretched across a pond on an island close to shore. The water was shallow enough to wade, so we investigated. By this time we had moved beyond our fear of exposing our bodies to the water. It seemed impossible to prevent getting it on us, so why try?

The men were crocodile hunting. They showed us the tracks and said that if they were lucky, the crocodile would be in the net within a couple of days. Men had been hunting crocodiles like this for six or seven thousand years. No change. No need to change. We drank tea with the men and ate stewed fish on their boat.

"We live on the Nile; all our lives are here, at this place," they said.

The scenery along the river was wonderful, a slow-moving phantasmagoria of sand dunes, palms, steep cliffs, banana trees, and brilliant colors as the sun changed position. In the evenings we watched the flight of cranes decorating the crimson glass of the river. We heard the constant sigh of the wind and the continuous chugging of water pumps.

People waved to us everywhere, and children ran along the banks to keep up with our boats. They had never seen kayaks before, but they were not frightened of them, or us, or anything that sailed on their great river. Villagers all along the Nile invited us ashore and into their houses to drink tea, to eat, to sleep, whatever we wanted. They were secure in their place on the river and had no fear of strangers.

It reminded me of the contentment that reigned in the great city built by Pharaoh Ramses I, as described by a thirteenth-century B.C. Egyptian poet.

Its fields are full of all good things and it has provisions and sustenance every day. Its channels abound in fish and its lakes in birds. Its plots are green with herbage and its banks bear dates. Its granaries are overflowing with barley and wheat and they reach unto the sky. Fruits and fish are there for sustenance and wine from the vineyards of Kamkeme surpassing honey. He who dwells there is happy; and there the humble man is like the great elsewhere.

One evening we found an island minutes before the sun dropped behind a nearby village, and Cherif paddled to the mainland to get bread and eggs while I set up camp. It was getting dark. I saw shadows in the water. A boat silently passed the island about fifty yards offshore. A man slipped stealthily off the back of the boat and started creeping along, half hidden by the stern. Thirty yards farther along, another man slipped into the water. It looked like a team of frogmen at work. They seemed to be watching me. It was too dark to make out their faces. I called out, "*Salaam aleikum,*" but there was no answer. This was curious. Where the hell was Cherif, who could talk to them at least? They were coming closer to the island. I was getting nervous. I yelled out for Cherif, and he answered from the darkness.

He paddled around the men, then said, "They say for you to stop shouting. You're scaring the fish."

Each night Cherif went through a religious ritual. It was infectious, and soon I too found myself facing the west at sunset every evening. Certainly my mind was becoming quieter as the journey continued. Being on the river all day was like meditating. I felt as if my identity were dissolving in the river. Also, I was able to previsualize to an astounding degree, looking further and further ahead. It was not the usual kind of anticipation—the I-can't-wait variety—but a sense of the Nile stretching from its mid-African sources clear through to the Mediterranean. I could see that our "goal" of kayaking the Nile was beside the point. We were doing it for the sake of doing it.

We labored at those kayak paddles like galley slaves. Often it was almost unbearably hot. If we craved ease, why did we act so? It was not ease we sought at all, but action that we wanted. Action for its own sake, because the idea of destination was slipping away from us. At the 500-mile mark neither of us really cared whether there was, in fact, a destination.

We were enveloped in the myths of antiquity, flanked by low, stark ruins in the empty desert. Near Dongola we came upon a team of Italian archaeologists from the University of Rome who were studying the Merowe Kingdom of around 500 B.C. We talked with them for a day and discovered that after spending six months digging in this utterly desolate place, where six mini-pyramids marked the center of the kingdom, they all were changed.

"A great peace, here in the desert," said the leader, a fifty-year-old professor from Florence.

"Why peaceful? Is it the silence? The people?" I kept firing questions at him.

"It is an absence," he said. "Something is missing. But it is something we don't need. We find ourselves walking miles in the evening, just to get to the river and watch its flow."

At the Merowe dig, in 100-degree heat, I ran from the river to the pyramids, making a game of it. A desert woman, entering into the spirit of the game, began running with me, laughing and dropping her belongings as she scampered along. We reached the first pyramid with me running backward and darting back and forth, the way the Plains Indians of America do their running. In a few minutes I was on top of the pyramid, where a bunch of Romans from the first century B.C. had scribbled their names. Then I was on top of a second pyramid, where I disturbed a giant eagle. It went winging off into the desert with an irritated scream. As I ran, I could hardly feel my shoulders and arms. I felt the air rushing in my nostrils, past my lungs and chest, as if the air were filling up my belly. The woman was screaming as she tried to keep up with me. Then I felt as though I were outside my body. Unlike other times, when I had felt I was riding above my shoulders and could see my body and the surroundings together, this time I felt I was in front of my forehead, between my eyebrows. Later I realized I had traveled in this space until I got back to the Nile, where the archaeologists were waiting.

"What did you do to that desert woman?" they asked. "We never saw one of those people running before."

The kayaking got easier every day. I felt as though I could paddle to America and wondered whether it would be possible. Too tough, though; there was no way to carry enough provisions. Maybe get supplies from ships accompanying the kayak? But that seemed like cheating. The dream popped as I focused on a four-thousand-year-old pyramid.

A few hundred miles before crossing the border into Egypt, we stopped at a Nubian village called Kerma and were greeted on the beach by a swarm of about fifty children. We walked barefoot out of the kayaks, through rocks, toward the chug-chug sound of motors running their irrigation system.

In the village we were invited to remain a while. "This is a holy place," the villagers said, "and you must stay here and feel its holiness in you."

In the last of the day's light we took a tour of the village.

It was very small. The doorways of the houses excited me because they were decorated with the glyphs and symbols of ancient Egypt. I saw the pictograph of Thoth over a doorway and asked if the man who lived there was a scholar. The villagers looked surprised. "You know that?" they asked. Inside some of the houses the people had painted the walls with Egyptian symbols. They did not know what half the signs meant; they just knew they had power. They used them in a talismanic way.

"Holy place, holy place," they kept saying.

The sun went down, very red and big, and we were taken to the home of a man named Mahomed Ali. Beds were set up for us, and dinner was served: a pancake-type bread atop a spicy sauce in a large enamel pan. Four of us ate from the pan, breaking off the bread and scooping out the sauce with our fingers. The meal was one of the best I've ever had.

In the morning our host was sad. "My grand uncle died in the night, so I cannot show you our home," he said. But one of his friends would show us the temple of an old king. They said that people came to this temple, burned incense before it, and the doors opened automatically. I got goose bumps when I went inside, and I spent time there alone, meditating.

This was no linear world in which I found myself. It was circular, like the ancient Egyptian concept of time and motion, like the passage of the sun god, Ra, around the earth. I was poised in the space and grip of the Nile, in touch with perhaps the most ancient source of power on earth.

Mahomed Ali's friend turned out to be a high official in the police department, a man everybody knew and depended upon. When people insisted that we could not kayak much farther because of a cataract downriver, he drove us in his Land Rover to the cataract so that we could make a decision. When we got there, we saw a huge statue lying on its back in the shallows, with its hands crossed over its chest. It looked as though it had drowned.

"The Persians were here," said the policeman, as if this had happened a few days ago, "and they tried to change everything." He was referring to the time of Darius, about 500 B.C., when the Persian Empire had ruled Egypt. I walked along the edge of the rapid, where the water was very shallow, then waded out a few hundred feet. Still too shallow.

We took a felucca to another section of the river. The water there moved at a very high speed just around the place we needed to shoot, and then smashed against a rock, sending up hissing, white spray.

"I'm not going down that channel for any money," said Cherif.

"There is another place," said the captain of the felucca, "but I will not take my boat there because of the current."

The spacing of rocks allowed me to reconnoiter by swimming. I slipped into the water and swam about a quarter of a mile, feeling the pull of the current—steady but not terribly strong. When I reached the place the felucca captain had referred to, it wasn't too bad. There was a kind of weir creating about a three-foot drop, and then a morass of boiling water. I clung to a black rock and eased along until I was even closer to the spot. Well, on second thought, it was not such a good-looking place. I wondered whether I should tell Cherif and then decided I would have to level with him.

On the way back to the village there was a lot of discussion about the rapids. We knew we could simply get a truck and drive straight to Wadi Halfa. From there we could cross Lake Nasser by steamer to get beyond the Aswan High Dam to the Nile's continuation. But we were reluctant to leave the river.

The felucca captain remained adamant. "Don't do the rapids," he said. "Too many bad things happen to people on the rapids."

David (this page) and Cherif (facing page), midway through the journey. DAVID SMITH.

I would have felt easier in my mind if I had been able to see the river from bank to bank. But it was so wide, so spread out, that there was no way of seeing it whole.

Without any further talk, we both realized that we felt compelled to shoot the rapids. Later the same afternoon Cherif and I were on the water, without any real plan, just being pulled along. We paddled until darkness, then moved into a fork that ended in a swampy, mosquito-infested cul-de-sac. I could almost feel the malaria in the air. We set up tents on a small beach and went to sleep with the roar of the rapids in our ears.

In the morning three boys and a woman paddled up in a felucca. The woman worked busily, cutting up greens, while the boys watched us arguing about whether we should hit the rapids.

"Ask them what they think," I suggested to Cherif, "and let's go with what they say."

It was a risk, but these were river people, not policemen, and I thought we might learn something.

Cherif agreed, and only minutes later we were approaching the rolling, churning white water. The river people said the water could be handled if we went with the right gods. Cherif asked if Hapi, the river god for whom my kayak was named, was one of them. They nodded their heads affirmatively. We were getting five-thousand-year-old power from the river.

It seemed to be calmer on the western side, and Cherif headed there. I went straight into the hot spot, yelling with excitement as I hit the churning water and went into the roller-coaster ride. A wall of white water loomed up and I shot skyward. I made it and flipped around in an eddy. Cherif was holding back. I waved, "Come on through." Then I waited half an hour.

There was a croc right alongside the kayak. I had always associated the beasts with still water, but later I learned that they often wait below rapids for food to wash through. I wondered how close I had come to being crocodile lunch. Finally Cherif came down. He had parked his kayak and scrambled over the rocks, just to check out whether it really was all right. I don't think he trusted my judgment after he had seen me disappearing into the white water. He had to make it on his own terms. I felt he had acquired a new identity on the river. He was more sensibly bold now, more intelligently cautious.

In a short while we were approaching the next rapids, the place I had reconnoitered by swimming the day before. It still looked bad. We parked the kayaks among some rocks and inspected it. "I thought you said it was a three-foot drop," said Cherif. Now it looked nearer to five feet. I was worried. It was vertical, and there were big rocks in the way. The turbulence lasted for only about fifty yards, though, and then the water smoothed out.

"We can do it," said Cherif firmly. We dug in our paddles and shot forward.

Later Cherif said, "The Sudanese exaggerate about things, don't they?"

We both smiled.

Still more rapids lay ahead, but for now we had reached

a stretch of quiet water, a haven. We passed close by beautiful, organic-looking sculptures of rock jutting upward; huge sand dunes and palm trees formed the shoreline backdrop. The wind was a whisper as we paddled along smoothly with the temperature steady at 106 degrees. Then I saw water collecting in the bottom of my boat. We found a beach, and I unloaded, washed my clothes, took a run, and then repaired the boat. Hapi had four bruises, three slashes, and a puncture. I patched the sensitive areas and packed up, and we were back in the water for an afternoon of traveling against the wind. It was now blowing strongly out of the Sahara. A sandstorm in the early evening kicked up such dense dust that we had to eat in the tent. We were running out of everything: sprouts, cheese, garlic, oil, and bread. We needed fresh food.

In the morning I ran five miles through the beautiful sand dunes, soft and shaped like a woman's breasts. Sometimes I sank into the sand up to my knees. I felt the sand loved me.

After breakfast we hit the last set of rapids. The danger was a matter of only minutes, but the Nile had changed for us. Early on, it had been a quiet friend, flowing us along; in the past two days it had shown another face. In my walk to Agadir I had always known that I could die, but the awareness that we could drown in the benign embrace of the river was somehow shocking.

A few hundred yards ahead of Cherif, I heard the roar. I saw the drop. The first fall plunged me a dozen feet, then the kayak rushed through another fifty feet of white water, bouncing wildly, its dowels cracking. Through a blaze of spray in the hot air I yelled, "Keep going, Hapi! Stick together, baby!" I was telling myself the same thing. When I could see again I looked to my right for Cherif, who was just entering the center fall. He stayed up for a few seconds, and then he was flipped over as if shot. I heard him yelling.

It was a mess. Cherif got to his overturned boat, and I

saw him struggling to the beach. I spun around, picking up his hat, canteen, date jars, shaving kit, plastic container, water pail, and some clay cooling jars. Eventually I got all the stuff together and made it over to the beach. Then I checked the boats again for holes. None. Good. There were some bad scrapes and broken wood on Cherif's, but the bottom of his boat was made of thick rubber. He said he had rolled over as soon as he hit the bottom of the spillway to avoid a rock. He got out from under the boat while he was still underwater and kept the boat off the rocks. He was very high.

"I remember every detail. After I got out I didn't let go. I was trying to stuff back the things that were coming out of the boat."

His rudder was bent, and he straightened it out with a rock.

I was high, too. I wanted to go back over that fall. I asked Cherif if I could use his kayak because it was empty.

"Are you serious?"

So I emptied Hapi and took her out. She felt very light all of a sudden. I started paddling toward the great spillway. But then something spoke to me: "You had your ride. Don't be greedy."

A few hours later we were back in the water, paddling against a bitterly cold north wind filled with sand. It was almost impossible to breathe. The sand got into everything. It was like a rain of tiny pebbles pattering against the skins of the kayaks. Once, in a rift in the murk, I saw a bird fishing in the shallows. Then it was blotted out by sand. It was all I could do to keep from being pushed back up the Nile. Ten minutes later there was another rift, and there was the same bird, standing on one leg, half-asleep. I had to use such force to keep the kayak into the wind that I wondered if the paddle would break. Another rift, and I saw Cherif on the east bank hauling his kayak on a rope.

On one of our last nights together on the river, we stopped at a village called Delgo, where, although many of the

Yoga at sunrise on the Nile. DAVID SMITH.

inhabitants were sick, a community dinner was held for us.
The villagers wanted to know about America.

"I hear the wages are high, but the responsibilities are
higher," said one man.

A man named Gumma asked me to dance and sing. I
did a Bobby Darin impression, singing "Clementine," and
then Johnny Ray, wailing "Cry." It was a very impassioned
performance. A huge man with a scarf around his waist beat
a large can for a drum as I danced a free-form African rock
and roll. I got them all interested in yoga, and half the
village did headstands. Then we played Frisbee by torch-
light. In the morning the sun rose from a horizontal slot of
brilliant carmine in the desert.

When we left the village all the people gathered, laughing and shouting, to say goodbye. We strangers to the river
had the drive to paddle from Khartoum to Cairo but could
not smile any wider or laugh any louder than these villagers
on the banks of the Nile.

Quite suddenly, as if we had been embraced by spirits, we were changed: a spell was broken, and everything was different. We could not describe it. It was not good, and it was not bad. I had an inspiration.

"Let's follow James Bruce," I said. "Abyssinian" Bruce, an eighteenth-century Scottish explorer, penetrated this part of Africa more deeply than any other European of his day, reaching the source of the Blue Nile and doing military service in an Abyssinian civil war, among other adventures. We had talked a lot about him during the trip. We decided to retrace a part of Bruce's overland journey, and took a truck for some hundred miles that he had walked. The truck brought us to Wadi Halfa; from there we embarked by paddle steamer on the thirty-hour trip across the length of Lake Nasser, to Aswan.

At Aswan it was as though we had run into a brick wall. After flowing down the river for so long, possessed by its timeless rhythms, we stumbled into the clangor of a dusty city in the sometimes frantic pursuit of serving its tourists. The beggars, the con men, the gleaming sightseeing buses, the towering hotels, were all set against the backdrop of the gigantic dam. Our first view of that immense concrete barrier struck us both mute for a long time. Eventually Cherif said, "Somehow, it doesn't belong there."

I knew what he meant. We went back to our Egyptian hotel, the Grand, and spent the evening in the bar, saying little, silently sipping cool drinks under an enormous moon.

"I guess that's it," said Cherif.

"You want to quit?" I asked.

"That dam is really the end of the Nile," he said. "They finished the river for me, at least the river we planned to kayak."

"I'm going to go on," I said.

"Oh, I am too," he said, "but I'm going to break the journey here for a while."

He was saying good-bye. We finished our drinks and went to our rooms.

The next day we walked down to the banks of the Nile together. I carried my kayak. Hundreds of people trailed along after us.

"Well," I said, shaking hands with Cherif, "I'll see you next time."

"I may overtake you," he said, taking my hand in a grip like a vise. We both laughed, then I shoved off.

Another hundred miles downriver I visited Luxor, the city of palaces in the Valley of the Kings. Only a few days after this brief contact with ancient royalty, a very contrasting visit brought home some of the harsher reality of present-day Egypt. I went to a hospital to get information about bilharzia. It was 100 degrees in the shade. Doctors dressed in three-piece suits sat on a muddy lawn, taking their coffee breaks. The place was filthy. I could not even accept a cup of coffee. A dentist was yanking sixty teeth an hour, no Novocain. Many of the patients had open sores or terrible coughs and were spitting blood. Although there was a lot of laughing and joking, one doctor told me that the most common disease in Egypt was not bilharzia or malaria but good old-fashioned depression. "They want things they can't have," he said, plunging a needle into another buttock.

A short time later I was again standing on the banks of the Nile. It was like glass. Hapi glided smoothly as I pushed off from shore. I was very content. I paddled twenty-seven hours without stopping to sleep, and during the night clouds covered the full moon. I had come almost stealthily upon a group of men at work in the middle of the Nile, clustered around the line of a long, sunken net. The men were totally absorbed, and after my experience of disturbing the work of fishermen, I was loath to shout. It was a mistake. The sleek line of my kayak must have been only a silent mark in the silver water as I slid past their limited view. But they saw me.

"Samak!" they shouted.

I figured that this meant "Are you fishing?"

But I couldn't say much more than "No!" which sounded dumb, so I didn't answer at all. Another mistake.

They yelled louder. I could feel the fear. After all, they had never seen a kayak before. What was it? And what was it doing here, in their fishing grounds? They were becoming angry. I could hear messages relayed from boat to boat. Who was this on their river?

Hapi was the fastest small boat I had seen on the Nile. I did not think they could possibly catch me. I stayed ahead of the shouts easily enough; then there was a silence. But as fast as I had slipped through the darkness, two boatloads of men suddenly appeared out of the gloom behind me. They were rowing explosively, two men on each oar, one pushing and the other pulling. It was their sprint team.

I had a split second to make up my mind. Run for it or face them? I wheeled and faced them. There was still a long way to go on this Egyptian Nile, and if it was going to be full of men wanting to kill me, I might as well confront them now. One man grabbed for my bow rope while another stood over me with a pole raised above his head and poised in a chopping position. He was the fish-scarer. I had seen these men smashing the surface of the Nile to drive the fish into nets, and the memory of the savage blows now drilled tiny electric needles into my skull.

As has happened to me before in moments of extreme danger, I perceived the next few seconds in slow motion. I felt suddenly confident and peaceful. I held up my hands in a position halfway between prayer and defense. I could almost smell the adrenaline flowing in the other fellow's veins. He kept making short, jerky fakes at my skull. I mustered up the most sincere *salaam aleikum* I had ever uttered. He relaxed and slowly lowered the pole an inch or two.

When they pulled the kayak to shore and got me out of it, I tried to make a connection with them. There was no Arabic from Cherif to smooth the way, but I thought of a substitute. I had won a medal for performing in the Suez

Canal marathon swim. Quickly I pulled the medal out of my pack and showed it to them. I said, "Abu Hief," the name of Egypt's greatest swimmer, and then, "*Adalla, adalla,*" the Arabic word for friend. I wanted them to know I was an athlete and a friend before trying to communicate, as best I could, that I was traveling from Khartoum to Cairo.

It worked. Within five minutes we all were drinking mint tea.

The Egyptian Nile was quite unlike the Sudanese Nile. It was the same river, but everything about it was different. It was a problem of numbers here: too many men were looking for too few fish. In *The White Nile*, Alan Moorehead noted the death motif of ancient Egypt: a pharaoh with his arm raised, about to club an enemy to death. Or a fisherman, I thought, about to strike a kayaker. Moorehead saw the same energy in the thrust of a riverside heron's beak, but rhythmic, poetic. I saw a flock of kites fighting viciously over some food in a field. Too many kites did not make a poetic image.

What the Nile journey was about—if it needed to have meaning—had become a conundrum. My intention was exposure to stress and to distance and to the desert, down 1700 miles of river. That was far enough to know why the journey had been made. But as I neared Cairo on a water highway now densely flanked by fellaheen working in checkerboard fields fenced by ditches of controlled Nile waters, I saw no terminus in my mind. Yet I would stop somewhere, and that would be the "end," in my Western way of thinking.

It had always been in the back of my mind to climb one of the great pyramids at Giza, and as it turned out, this marked the symbolic end of the Nile journey.

The face of Cheops' pyramid, ten miles west of Cairo, was far from smooth. After a thirteenth-century earthquake cracked the face, the builders of nearby cities had used the pyramid as a quarry for the Tura limestone that once covered it. Some of the blocks at the base were as big as I was, and I had to use my arms to pull myself up. I zigzagged, keeping up a rhythm that was like running.

I was climbing on a monument that had taken twenty years and the sweat of twenty thousand to build. It was an ascent out of one consciousness and into another. The city of Cairo showed faintly, its towers and minarets rising from the pollution. I could see half a dozen more pyramids at Memphis and Saqqara. I sat down cross-legged on the square platform that was created when the triangular cap of the structure was stolen away; I gazed out into the Sahara.

I had never seen such a grand view of my planet. I no longer felt the burning rays on my almost black skin. Ra's sun spun overhead and then down toward the sands to the west, toward Morocco, where I had first felt the presence of the source on land.

The sun of this land was life-giving; the ancients lived by it, sustained by the sun god, Ra, who gave them greatness in accord with their great river. Let the light shine through. Use the sun.

I fell into a meditation. Soon darkness had stolen up the slopes of the pyramid without my sensing the true end of day.

As I came out of the meditation, a message came to me. "Heal."

Chapter 6

Earth Adventure

We had been driving for an hour on Interstate 80, the highway running east-west through northern New Jersey. The van was stifling in the 90-degree June heat, and the motor was overheating. John Davenport, the tall, skinny counselor driving the van, was from Bangor, Maine, and he was not used to this kind of heat. "Whew," he said, wiping his forehead, "what's it going to be like out in the woods?" I sat next to him, trying to figure out how I would handle the next few days. Behind us, in three rows of seats, was a group of young people suffering from schizophrenia in various stages of development and seriousness, people whom society is prone to regard as "crazies."

But to me they were also something much more significant: they were the people of tomorrow.

Schizophrenia is the phenomenal mental ailment of our age, prevented from nearly disabling the society only by the widespread use of medication. Most disturbing of all, the illness seems to me to be caused in large part by the basic structure of our society, which stimulates schizophrenic response. The stresses of modern human life demand fast, even immediate adaptation to changing conditions. But society's rules, regulations, and manners are still jogging along about half a century behind.

A certain empathy for schizophrenics is necessary in any dealings with them. I had been brought close to a state of schizophrenia myself by an immense gulf between me and the "normal" world. I led a kind of life that did not much resemble that lived by anyone else. Perhaps all athletes feel this in an out-of-shape civilization. I was not, of course, schizophrenic in a clinical sense; but, like these sufferers in the van, I had developed a double set of reactions to the world, one based on my discovery of the source and the other focused on dealing with those who had not discovered it.

I was in the van, planning an expedition into the wilderness, in the role of consultant to what has been called a "healing community." This was a unique nonprofit enterprise called Earth House, located near Princeton, New Jersey, offering a "holistic and orthomolecular" design for recovery from major mental disorders of many kinds. Its staff does not regard major mental disorders as the result of a "split" in personality, but rather as a disorder of perception in which the sufferer has been made "nonordinary" by the strain of trying to conform to impossible situations.

Earth House was founded in 1970 by Rosalind LaRoche, a niece of Rosalind Russell. LaRoche, a graduate of Sarah Lawrence, was a recovered schizophrenic herself. As a colleague of Dr. Carl Pfeiffer, director of the Brain Bio-Center in Princeton, she had treated thousands of schizophrenics, some to spectacular recoveries and many to profoundly changed, functioning lives. She had tapped me years before when I was passing through New York on my way to Africa, her attention caught by my talk of the "holistic athlete, who gets his performance from the earth."

"We believe that the conventional methods of treatment are running out of energy," she said. "Can you help us?"

Immediately behind me in the van sat Rob, a porky, sullen, twenty-four-year-old chronic depressive who, before we left Earth House, had said, "I won't be able to do this today. I'm sorry." But he was on his way, though he looked ready for Death Row—morose, grimly resigned, and bitterly opposed to the kind of change we were seeking in this expedition.

At one of our rest stops he came up to me, his face twitching; he hunched his shoulders forward in a convulsive shrug and said, "I'm going to do everything possible to sabotage this foolish idea."

"It's going to surprise you," I said.

"You'll be okay, Rob," said John Davenport.

To get schizophrenics into touch with the primal energies of the wilderness is not easy. They live primarily in their minds and are rarely conscious of their bodies. Most are in a state of complete rejection of society, and the wilderness is an almost unthinkably threatening extension of the towns and cities in which they live.

But I believed completely, from the Sierra Nevada days with my father and more recent experience, that the wilderness "heals," if only because it is one of the few places on earth that simply leaves you alone to be yourself. My mission was to persuade my charges that the wilderness we were entering did not faintly resemble the ghastly "wilderness" of the spirit in which they suffered out their lives.

Rosalind had wanted me to put together an exercise program for the "students" (as they are called at Earth House) that would boost the effects of their specially fortified diets and nutrient therapies. Though Rosalind was not an athlete, she had learned, as an athlete learns, that both identity and action are closely linked to nutrition. The body is a fantastic instrument for rectifying the mistakes of bad diet, but every response it so makes must consume energy needed for other adaptations. Long-term bad diet produces long-term sickness of some kind or another, if not premature death.

Therefore it was easy for me to cooperate with Rosalind's ideas of diet and exercise. The wilderness exposure component was an idea that developed out of the exercise program we set up. It was a natural step from beginning to heal the students' bodies to giving them an objective challenge that would entail a measure of stress in a relatively unthreatening environment. Earth House was close to both city and wilderness. The Delaware Valley and its broad, slowly flowing river were a short drive from Rosalind LaRoche's nineteenth-century farmhouse headquarters. So the Earth Adventures were born.

Behind Rob sat Monty, expressionless and totally silent; he was nearly catatonic. Monty had attempted suicide twice—once from a window (broken pelvis, arms, shoulder, and ribs) and once with a knife (fifty-six slashes of the inner arms and a deep stab wound in the chest).

Next to Monty was JC, a compulsive, six-pack-a-day smoker who had known little but hospitals for years. He was dark and attractive, twenty-six, and he was rocking slightly and humming to himself. Every now and then he stabbed his right hand into thin air before his face in a snatching motion that looked like catching invisible flies. He wore a wool-knit longshoreman's cap. His down jacket, which he refused to take off, was stained with sweat. JC was very disturbed, and I had been forced to confiscate from him a pint of heavy cream, which he had been trying to drink surreptitiously. I persuaded him to drink fruit juice instead. He was also chewing tobacco.

Behind JC, in the middle of the third row of seats, was Susie, a manic-depressive and member of one of America's most distinguished and wealthy industrial families. She was in her mid-twenties, a wistful-looking and somewhat hollow-cheeked girl, but attractive. Next to Susie sat twenty-two-year-old Kate, who was strikingly beautiful but badly overweight.

In the back seat were Barbara, a sad and terrified girl of twenty-three who had attempted suicide three times; Peter, who was underweight and a manic-depressive; and a Venezuelan named Juan, a catatonic schizophrenic whose father, uncle, and grandfather all had committed suicide. Despite the differences in their illnesses, these three often behaved as a group. In the van they had locked arms and were rocking slightly, although not consciously, in unison.

"I'm just too sick to go, don't you see?" said JC. I grinned encouragingly at him.

But encouragement is only the nonschizophrenic's notion of the helping hand. Both Davenport and I had to steel ourselves not to try and do the "human" thing of reducing pressure on them. We must seek instead to increase the stress of the environment, in the way I had been shown in the Pioneer Program and as Cherif and I had experienced during the Nile trip, in which vigorous and decisive action comes naturally out of the need to cope with stress. But it had to be stress that we thought we could master, as exemplified by us facing the Nile rapids.

Though an Earth Adventure looked simple, it wasn't. Each one involved months of preparation. In exercise classes and on preliminary hikes I had shown the participants how to modify a mental state through physical effort. Breathing was important. Calisthenics toned the body. I knew these people and their personal histories before we set out.

Only the aim of an Earth Adventure was simple. Get the schizophrenics as far away as possible from society. Get them out of their ruts of gloom, their dependencies on antipsychotic medication. Get the world in which they suffered out of sight and as much out of mind as possible.

"Stop the van!" Barbara screamed suddenly. "I've got to throw up!"

Unless they were hopelessly depressed, they would do almost anything to get attention. The ultimate bid was to swan-dive out a window, as one van traveler had attempted.

They were creatures who sought love but who might not know it when they encountered it. Their parents probably had loved them, but there had been slips in the cosmic scheme. In some cases overstressed parents broke down or ran away or killed themselves, leaving their children with a sense of resignation to the arbitrariness of fate. Other youngsters seemed almost genetically incapable of accepting love, driving their parents wild with despair.

Could these disturbed men and women find in the wilderness a missing ingredient in their lives? Or were they forever beyond the capability of the rest of us to reach them? There was no sickness in the wilderness. There was instead a chance to find their own authority in the stillness of the woods.

In the "civilized" world, of course, these people had no authority. They had defense postures or reflexes or just plain twitches, which, they had learned, had fancy Latin names. When things got too tough for them, they fell down and screamed, or went to bed sulking or depressed, or drank a bottle of cream or Lysol, or swallowed an overdose of any number of drugs. Even their concepts of sickness itself were not their own.

Barbara was actually vomiting outside the van. Davenport stood nearby, watchfully. Clearly she was distressed and frightened; she might even really have been sick. But the odds were that she wasn't.

From the start the image of wilderness was negative in their minds. Most of the Earth Adventure participants had a downright dread and suspicion of all wild places. Bugs, snakes, mosquitoes, rain, wind, cold, damp—the picture of wilderness was entirely negative for people who had learned that they should have warmth, comfort, drugs, and others serving them hand and foot. At the beginning of each trip I had to indoctrinate myself. I could not be sucked backward into their quagmire. I had to say to myself: "These people are sick, sure, but they are also indulgent, self-pitying, self-deceiving, and, in my everyday view of things, dishonest. They will, in the next few days, do everything in their power to blame me for everything that goes wrong for them."

Most conventional methods of treating sick people are hindered by unspoken acceptance of the belief that they are "guilty" of being sick. The people who have set themselves up as healers judge the sick from the moral standpoint of the healthy, and the prevailing notion that blame can somehow bring about "improvement" is a hard one to fight.

The Earth House philosophy hinges on using the natural energy of the schizophrenics to overcome the acquired lack of energy. The trick is to find a positive way of releasing the energy that is locked up inside them, or is being dissipated in destructive and negative action. It takes a certain amount of nerve to do the opposite of conventional treatment in these cases. My idea was to let the group loose in an environment that was not in itself going to hurt them. If they got hurt, they would have done it to themselves. Nobody would be blaming them there. If there was going to be blame, they would have to place it on themselves. If there was judgment, then it must be self-evident that the judge and the judged were the same person.

We reached the Delaware Water Gap, that cliffed narrowing of the river where wild and rocky terrain has prevented farming and commercial development.

"In a little while," I told the group, "we are going to be leaving all this familiar countryside behind and entering the beginnings of the wilderness. This is not a frightening place. But you have got to take it seriously and pay attention to it because we are going into high places, and if you fall, you will be hurt."

"I'm not doing any climbing, and that's that," said JC, shaking his head and jerking at a couple of invisible flies.

"I've got no head for heights," whispered Barbara.

Monty secretively touched his still-healing lacerations on both wrists, likely inflicted by a hunting knife and unlike the thin razor slashes of most attempted suicides.

"I want to go to Boston," he muttered. His consuming ambition was to reach Boston, buy a gun, put it in his mouth, and blow out his brains.

Fear of the natural wilderness is tied to a mental wilderness where terrible things will surely occur or, worse yet, are planned. I made no effort to quell the group's fears. In fact, the more frightened they were, the better, because their later "conquest" of the wilderness would then be their first great victory over themselves.

"We are going to be doing certain things," I said. "Anybody who hangs back may spoil it for the others. This is a group effort."

To achieve the right balance between freedom and discipline was the nub of a successful Earth Adventure. Was I to be an authority figure? A parent? The exemplar of all hopes? Ideally they should first trust me, then begin to make a kind of transference to me, as a patient might to a psychoanalyst. Of course, there was never enough time for this to develop fully, but I had another ace card to play—my technical proficiency in the things we were about to do. In one place we would visit—a long, tree-flanked stretch of sometimes glass-smooth lake water called Sunfish Pond— I would plunge in and swim the full length of the lake and then back again. It would serve as a dynamic example of proficiency, freedom, mastery of the water, and the capability of the individual to move without encumbrance. Usually, after such swims, all my fellow adventurers plunged in and thrashed around. It did not matter how unskilled they might be in the water. They had seen how things could be.

When we arrived at the campsite, which was off the main road at the top of some vertical bluffs thickly swathed in oaks and walnuts and overlooking the Delaware River, I got them out of the van immediately and hustled them along.

"Let's go, let's go!" I cried. I wanted to confuse them, not give them time to brood on the strangeness of their surroundings. They must be kept moving, so that at the end of their confusion they would discover they had actually done something.

They found themselves on a narrow trail and moving fast, grumbling. The woods on either side were impenetrable, and only the distant songs of birds told them that any other living thing was present. Dressed in a track suit, I jogged back and forth beside them, giving them my spiel. "You're out of shape right now," I said. Most were tranquilized, and exercise had to work against the medication in them. "But once the blood starts to flow, you'll feel it in your head. You'll feel tired for a bit, but then the energy will start to flow and you'll feel terrific. Keep at it real steady. Don't force yourselves." I had to laugh at myself for saying that. They rarely forced themselves to do anything.

Most Earth House patients were in poor physical condition when they arrived at Earth House. But this group was in really bad shape. The uncoordinated limbs, the sagging faces, the hopeless, wounded eyes, the beer belly on JC, the sunken cheeks on Rob—all indicated hard times ahead.

Barbara was trembling even as she walked. It was a procession of pure pain on the hoof. And there was this healthy-looking fellow running up and down beside them. But that was the point. I could do it. I was something else —healthy, fit, competent. They would follow me.

In the human mind, for some reason, the act of following is more easily performed when it is associated with climbing. Most of our language dealing with the idea of accomplishment has to do with "climbing" to success, "scaling" new heights, "surmounting" obstacles, "rising" through the ranks, even though no actual ascent of the body, or perhaps even the mind, takes place. We were literally climbing now because my followers had been taught to believe that by climbing they were somehow going to a better place. The biblical mountain is in our psyches, and they did not have to be Bible readers to know that Moses brought the Ten Commandments down from the mountain, or that you have to be on a mountain to know what a plain looks like. We were climbing from the plain now, and they knew that, felt it with apprehension. They knew they would have to face that rock cliff.

Once a fat and rather pathetic teenager named Bob got stuck on an Earth Adventure climb. He had fastened himself to the rock face and started weeping helplessly. I felt impelled to help him, but I held off for a moment, and I saw him watching me covertly. So I let him weep. It took about five minutes of tears on his part and talk on mine before he made a supreme effort and climbed to the top. The effort brought tears to my eyes.

"Hey, hey, look at me!" he cried. He raced around the top of the rock face so rapturously I thought he was trying to fly. Which perhaps he was.

Within the demands of the wilderness situation are contained the ingredients of personal salvation. But a hairline separates healthy stress and unhealthy stress. No manual will ever designate it by degree. It is measured instead by the immediate response of each individual to each kind of stress. The Canadian physician Hans Selye, who has written extensively about the effects of stress, has shown that when the capability to adapt to a situation is not known, or is denied, then collapse and even total breakdown, suicide, can follow the imposition of stress. Conversely, when the capability to adapt is known, then practically nothing will break down the person. Bob had had this capability. But then, in many different ways, so did they all. How might each find it?

The trail upward was chosen with much care, so that it would include enough physical challenge to control boredom but would not be so tough as to discourage them. This was the hardest part of my planning. It was all too easy to evaluate athletic effort in my own terms and forget that these people were physical wrecks. Yet who knew the exact point of breakdown, that moment when discouragement overtook challenge? Perhaps all of us were uncertain about treating the sick, for fear we would push them over the edge and so be responsible. Coddling was safer than challenging.

"I'd like you all to imagine that we are in central India now," I said to my sagging troops, "and the peacocks are screaming the warning that a tiger is somewhere in the vicinity. To be safe, we should try to reach the next ridge as soon as possible. From there we can get a clear view of the land and see if the big cat is close."

With that, I let out my notion of a peacock's scream. It was a cracked screech that sent some genuine American songbirds fleeing for higher branches.

"At the ridge," I puffed, "we all rest and consider our next move."

Objective, challenge, stress. The wreckage obediently lurched into faster motion. Some had brains; some had potentially good bodies. They wanted to be well, didn't they? They wanted to feel good, didn't they? But the weight of history was thousands of tons on their shoulders. Barbara, predictably, began to whine.

"I can't do it, I can't do it."

I saw that Monty was stone-faced, unreachable. I took Juan and JC, the first people in the route march, aside and said, "See if Barbara needs help." Juan dropped back, and Barbara, humiliated—she had eyed Juan earlier—speeded up before he could reach her. JC, on the other hand, looked confused. He clearly did not understand what was happening to him. Help Barbara? He was terrified of girls. Meanwhile, Rob's face was scarlet, not from exertion—he was in better shape than most of the others—but from rage. He felt he was being put on but could not figure out how to get through to me that he's the one who should be asked to do such jobs.

There was always a group dynamic to the Earth Adventures. Each one (I have led twelve in all) was different. There was no textbook or set of rules governing the behavior of these schizophrenic adventurers. Each group, as well as each individual within the group, had to be treated on the basis of how they responded to new situations, not on any preconceptions I might have had.

At this moment the group was behaving in response to a physical insult to their bodies. The overweight girl, Kate, had screwed up her face to cope with the agony of her pudgy muscles. Pete was becoming visibly depressed, his body bowed nearly double in its acceptance of his mind trip, which said, "Quit!" Juan was blank as a wall and moving like an automaton. Soon, I knew, he would walk into trees or over the edges of cliffs if he were not watched. He simply would not care until something wakened him. But I noticed that Monty had been moving steadily. It seemed to me that he had become stronger, more open to the rest of us.

Soon we would be at the ridge. It really wasn't that far. We stopped for a few minutes so the hikers could catch their breath and to enjoy a magnificent view. I pulled out a small pair of field glasses and looked down on the deliberately chosen vista that lay before us. We looked right down on the Water Gap itself, down toward rapids rushing between cliffs. A hermit thrush caroled nearby.

"What's that?" screamed Barbara, falling into the undergrowth. A cock pheasant clattered away into the blue sky.

"Are there snakes?" panted JC.

"I'm scared of heights," whimpered Kate.

To this group, it must be remembered, we were traversing the outer limits of hell, a nonurban environment infested with spiders, bugs, and snakes.

"The tiger has retreated," I said, "and we are safe for the time being."

"All this crap about tigers!" shouted JC. "I'm sick of it!"

"I kinda like the idea of there being a tiger," said Pete, snapping his head up for a second. "I mean, there really isn't a tiger, is there? It's just David's story, isn't it?"

There was a long silence. It was beautifully peaceful. John Davenport moved quietly through the group, tightening straps and checking packs and water bottles.

"All right!" I shouted suddenly. "Everybody on their feet. Let's move out!"

"What's this? A John Wayne movie?" complained Susie.

"It's Adolf Hitler in charge," said JC.

The groans and moans were drowned in the bustle of getting our stuff together, along with my running spiel about what we were going to do next.

The slope we were ascending was symbolic of the uphill journey that was their lives. If they could make this association and conquer the physical obstacles, perhaps the mental barriers would also be diminished. That is the beauty and the strength of symbolic action. I would reinforce this idea at every step of our climb.

After another fifteen minutes the group was exhausted, and we were still ten minutes from the ridge. I wanted to create a diversion that would snap them into fresh action and awareness. I decided to pose a real challenge: abandonment. I sprinted ahead of them and disappeared among the trees. What would they do? Retreat back down the trail? Huddle together and cry out for help? The schizophrenic may give up instantly, like young Bob on the rock face, as long as he is being watched; so I made sure I was out of sight of the group before I slowed down. When I reached the ridge, I settled myself on a rock and gazed outward from the almost vertical cliffs overlooking the Delaware River.

Would they keep moving? Could they find leadership in themselves, enough to force on?

Barbara was the first to straggle into view. Then the rest of the group dribbled onto the ridge. They looked sheepish at the discovery that there had never been any intention of abandoning them. Then they looked apprehensive: here on the mountain might await a nightmare they had not foreseen. They might actually succeed in reaching the top. "This all makes me feel sick," said Kate, in a faint, lost voice.

"Get the packs undone and the gear laid out," I said. "We'll be camping here for the night."

As usual, this was the ritualistic center of the Earth Adventure. Amidst the initial chaos of attempting to cope with collapsing tents, slipped guy wires, tent pegs that would not hammer in, and pillows that would not inflate, the adventurers began to develop a sense of themselves as a group and of what they could accomplish by working together.

We plunged into it. In the middle of the group John Davenport was supervising, a tent rose like a ship under sail, then collapsed on three people inside. John turned it into a joke. JC got one guy rope around his ankle, and Monty somehow got the other end around his, and they twanged together in a Chaplinesque scene. There was a whinny of pain when a mallet hit flesh instead of a peg, and a swoosh-hiss as a burgeoning wood fire went out when hit by some drinking water.

Daylight waned. Then there was a sudden surprise among the group when the camp was finally made, and a sense of satisfaction at having finished the work we had set for them. I always chose this time carefully, for sunset is a very important time in the wilderness. The fear of night is approaching, but the friendliness of day is still with you. It is a time for reflection and preparation for what lies ahead. Later that night, around the campfire, we would observe a timeless ritual: the telling of stories illuminated by the memories of nature.

Each Earth Adventure was an attempt to distill a simple truth from a complex problem. The sensory stimulation of these people was so tumultuous that none of them could have been expected to respond fully to the wilderness. Still, there was much they might learn. I recalled my father's words: "Remember, it is all in the details. Watch for the details; observe and remember them."

The advice is as old as our memories. The wilderness gives you all the information that you need to survive. This information is pouring in all the time—the placement of a squirrel's nest, the peel of a piece of bark, the hum of a certain kind of insect, the color of the dawning sun—but because we are so far removed from our primal landscape, we no longer receive its messages. They have to be learned afresh.

For the Earth Adventurers, terrified in the thickets of ignorance, the wilderness must be kept at bay if not denied or rejected. While John Davenport attended to the details of managing camp, it was my task to get the group to end their denials and face the wilderness challenge, thereby building confidence. It would be a step toward facing the personal demons they had been trying to lock out.

That night I decided to work on their fear of being alone in the darkness. "Let's do the Star Wars game," I said to John. It was played with flashlights and combined team hide-and-seek and tag. The game helped the adventurers get used to the dark without the overwhelming terror of the unknown dominating their minds. My last words to them before the fire was extinguished and goodnights said were, "In the morning we are going to learn something new about ourselves, and we will never be the same again."

In the evening messages of encouragement and optimism are in order. In the morning maximum stress and challenge are the rule. Even so-called healthy people have all their defenses up and operating by the afternoon. It is hard to get through with any really good learning after midday. But in the morning, particularly within the first hour of wakening, a person's defenses are not fully erected. I had found that if I stressed the Earth Adventurers correctly, when they were receptive to a swirl of new learning experiences, I could keep their defenses down for several hours. It is no accident that the most significant propaganda messages in totalitarian countries are broadcast first thing in the morning, while people are awakening.

Before first light I heard the sound of chopping. Incipient superman Pete was working away with his axe, proving that he was first, best, and brightest. On my earlier trips, when I was learning how to handle Earth House people, I kept the axe in my tent. I assumed that a schizophrenic with an axe must be dangerous. Rarely, this might be true. But this morning Pete was speaking to all of us. Nobody would leave the campsite without seeing what he had chopped.

I roused the others at first light, around five thirty— the hour of the firing squad for them—and got them going. This was difficult. Some of them had had problems getting to sleep and were exhausted from the strife of their hyperactive minds. Rob's plan to resist everything was already in shambles, and his moroseness had been replaced by apprehension. This could come, I knew, from the fear that he might be starting to feel better. Barbara's terror of heights had given way to her stronger fear of the dark. JC would not be stabbing for imaginary flies today; he'd be too busy trying to save his own ass. Susie would be recovering her aplomb and working on Monty. If Pete hummed tuneless songs this day, it would only be because he had momentarily forgotten that he was the Great Axeman.

Each Earth Adventurer was demonstrating that the effect of the wilderness was textural. It came out of the response of the individual to it. Each person was being fused into a common energetic of place and experience, and the neurotic self gave way step by step. The wilderness communicated through the collective memory of the species. It invoked a glittering campfire of the mind, with sabertooths lurking at the edges of darkness. The wolf howled in New Jersey. If I had postulated all this from an armchair it would have been totally incredible. There was no way I could turn it into a theory or a philosophy or any scheme of thought. It had to be lived.

The mind moved toward the source.

By now the adventurers knew they were engaged in a journey of epic importance. They were heroes, without yet being able to understand this. Joseph Campbell, in *The Hero with a Thousand Faces*, describes such a journey: "A hero ventures forth from the world of common day into a region of supernatural wonder; fabulous forces are encountered and a decisive victory is won; the hero comes back to bestow boons on his fellow men." I suppose I related to that and wanted to share the experience.

The place I had chosen for a "supernatural" experience for the group—a communion really—was utterly secluded. Walnuts and sycamores formed a canopy over our heads, and warblers darted through high branches. The Delaware River rapids murmured low in the background. To get there we had to descend two slopes. I chose Monty to go first. He had been a Big Ten pole-vault champion and should remember about heights and risk.

As Monty grabbed the nylon rope, the sun caught the lacerations on his wrists and inner arms up to the elbow. He had also slashed his inner thighs from groin to knee. The newly healed scars and stitches looked like zippers in his skin.

"I don't get it," he was saying. "What is this crap?"

"You just let yourself down backward," I said, "with me holding this rope."

"Trust you to hold me?" he said incredulously. "Are you crazy?"

"Even if you fell," John Davenport pointed out, "you wouldn't even bruise yourself." It was true. The slope behind him, while rocky, was about as steep as a mountain road for automobiles. Grumbling, Monty went down, backward. The others followed.

"This isn't so high," said Barbara brightly.

It has been said that schizophrenia is both an inward

and a backward journey. It seeks to recover that which has been, and so is essentially a mission of rediscovery. Disintegration has occurred, and reconstruction must occur in an uncluttered place. The wilderness awaits.

The second slope was tougher, involving a vertical drop of about six feet but ending on a grass bank that did not look frightening. Only Barbara balked at this. "I can't do it," she said.

"You must volunteer yourself," I said, "to make the change that you seek. Do you want to get well?"

Barbara looked at me, her lips quivering. "That's unfair," she said.

"The others are waiting," I said. She eased herself down.

In the event of outright failure at any point during an adventure, nothing was said or done, but the failed adventurer had to join the others by an easier route. In all the trips I supervised, I never went back to Earth House with a totally failed adventurer. Each traveler changed as a result of the journey he or she made.

Within an hour we were all at the bottom of the slope and ready for a period of rest and quiet reflection. We sat in a circle. There was a new spirit among us, a new openness to our surroundings. Everybody was a success. There was a tendency to smile. Story-telling time.

"One of my heroes is Knud Rasmussen, the great Danish scholar and adventurer," I began. "Between 1921 and 1924 he walked over land and ice from Greenland to Alaska, a distance of more than two thousand miles. He made the same kind of journey that you are making now, finding out about himself. But he was also a very inquisitive fellow, and he never lost a chance to talk to all the people he met along the way."

"They must have been Eskimos," said Kate.

"Right," I said. "And they taught him many things. One young Caribou Eskimo, who later became a shaman, was troubled by some terrifying and puzzling dreams he was having. Today I suppose we would say that he was emotionally disturbed or was going crazy. An old shaman prescribed a cure for him, and a tough one it was. There was no compassion or sympathy or care for this young sufferer. Instead he was ordered out into the wastelands in the middle of the Arctic winter night. There he had to sit cross-legged in a tiny igloo. He was told what to think. The old shaman said, 'Think only of the Great Spirit,' then he left the young man for thirty days. Occasionally scraps of food were brought to him. He suffered terribly. He told Rasmussen, 'I feel I died a little.' "

My people were totally caught up in the story. The voice of a wood thrush fluted beyond the murmur of a nearby stream.

"But, you see, intense concentration on the Great Spirit always brings a reward. It is a focusing of self made possible by isolation in a wilderness; there is no bad news out there. After a month, a friendly spirit arrived. It took the form of a woman who hovered in the air above the young Eskimo. He reached for her; but she disappeared, and he never saw her again."

"A friendly spirit?" asked Kate.

"She was his helping spirit thereafter," I went on. "I'd say that in his solitude he created her from the matrix of his own needs and made her his sworn helper. Later he fasted for another five months as he refined his wilderness experience into a new scheme of life. In this way he attained a knowledge of what he called the 'hidden things.' "

"I like to be alone," said Juan, "but I'd be frightened of the Great Spirit."

"Five months fasting," cried Susie. "I'd die!"

"Fasting can be a way of changing yourself," I said. "You see the body change itself, and your attitude toward it changes. The point of the young Eskimo's story is that the solution to the greatest problems is never instantly available. Anyway, he told Ramussen later that he had discovered the great secret of life. 'The only true wisdom,' he said, 'lives far from mankind, out in the great loneliness, and can be reached only through suffering. Privation and suffering alone open the mind of a man to all that is hidden to others.' "

Sufferers themselves, experts in pain and loneliness, they sat transfixed.

"Now let's go climb," I said, getting up.

I had chosen this slope because, like the rest of the adventure, it was deceptive. The climbers could not see the summit, and I would not be visible to them for much of the time. But each climber would be in full view of those waiting to climb. The stimulus would be coming from the group below rather than from me, the leader, above them.

And so began the individual crises that would set the tone of the rest of the Earth Adventure. Monty, climbing first, was fast and confident and eager, until he reached a smooth outcrop that looked easy from below but appeared insuperable once the climber got his hands to it. He vacillated back and forth for a while, and the group heard him mutter, "Oh, boy, this is a real bummer!" Surreptitiously he tried to tug the harness rope so I would give him a pull, but I did not respond. He clawed at the safety rope eventually, knowing this would reveal him to the others but figuring by that time that it was better to climb at any cost than to stall in disgrace. In a few minutes he was at the top, full of super-confidence.

"A breeze," he said.

Each climber faced the weakness in himself or herself that had led each of them to this place. Kate cried and refused to move. Barbara screamed for help, then went over the rock barrier like a monkey. Juan said nothing and came straight up. When nobody attended Susie, she too climbed, and with an energy and power that none of us suspected was in her. Pete tried to deny that the barrier was there; he said he had done this so many times before that it was

A group of Earth Adventurers and counselors at the Delaware Water Gap; Rosalind at center in dark sweater. DAVID SMITH.

dumb. Then he fell because of his phony confidence. In the silence that followed he climbed again and made it.

When we all were standing together again, after Pete had arrived with a whoop and a holler, everybody was smiling. It was infectious. For a moment I was tempted to pause and ruminate and talk it over. But schizophrenia remains schizophrenia. This was but a lull in their illness, and challenge would keep the demons at bay for a while. Tonight the demons would be back. Their dreams might be horrific.

The dreams, though, could be seen as part of the recovery that I hoped the adventure might initiate. I had been impressed during other Earth Adventures with how similar were their dreams to the dark, chaotic, even terrifying imagery of primitive people, as expressed in their myths and legends. James Frazer's *Golden Bough* is filled with stories that the schizophrenics related as dreams. It seemed to me that primitives and schizophrenics were seeking, through catharsis, a rebirth or return journey. In a myth, the traveler's journey leads back to reality; in an Earth Adventure, to health.

We went to sleep exhausted from the day. Groans told of the dreams. Usually at night we played charades, told stories, and made music with African beats. But this night the camp had been silent at eight o'clock. It would take time for the wilderness to effect change in the systems of these wounded travelers.

In the ensuing days we swung through the different layers of the adventure. There are no simple remedies for the human condition. The "cures" have to be as labyrinthine as the ailments. In the "forced march," which I devised for the afternoon of the third day, we were play-acting again—trying to escape a storm that was supposed to overwhelm us if we did not reach a certain point, a ravine between two high ridges, by a designated time.

Rage began to build as we traversed the rough country—a hillside, thickly forested lowlands, a stream winding for a mile, and then a steep climb. The rage grew out of the growing proximity of their real feelings.

"I haven't told you about my sister," said JC, "and how I planned to get even with her. She was such a bitch. She deserved to die. The only way I could control myself with her was to become depressed and drop out. Then to kill myself."

"I stood at the window on Times Square," said Monty. "There was this large billboard there, with a man blowing enormous smoke rings over the people. There were dope peddlers down there, and prostitutes, and barkers trying to get people into topless bars. I knew what I was doing. But when I held my arms in front of me, I couldn't hold them steady. I felt out of my body.

"I remember saying 'sick' a few times. I was sweating and nauseated. It was really bad. I don't remember jumping. But I crashed through a marquee down there, and that broke my fall. I was badly hurt but all right."

"My father had sex with me until I was sixteen," said Susie. "Then I realized I didn't have to do it, and I was strong enough to resist him. He beat me so badly that I ended up in the hospital. He went to prison, and my mother ran away to California."

Juan was awake, and a changed personality. He was fighting with Pete.

When consciousness is heightened, energy flows. Gaps in the action brought fights. At rest stops the group no longer fell into apathetic rest. They sprawled down, but their eyes were bright and challenging. They sometimes quarreled. This was a release of the aggression rising out of them. But they were also gaining confidence. Their minds were in a new kind of turmoil. The propaganda of society was silent, and this eventually became threatening. What, then, were they fighting against? Their own pasts were held in abeyance. There was a chance they could be competent. It was frightening.

The front cavern of the schizophrenic mind is filled with the fantastic. Reason, logic, and common sense have been replaced by the disorders of paranoia and all kinds of disrupted perceptions. Inevitably these found expression.

"Let's hurt that bird!" shouted Kate, pointing to a sparrow.

For "bird," substitute "society" or "people" or anybody. The schizophrenic slumbers under the cloak of such repression that almost any view under the robe is frightening.

When the going got too tough, the emotions frothing too high, we played games. "Capture the flag" put the adventurers out in the undergrowth, where they were woodsmen or freedom fighters who had to penetrate hostile territory ahead and seize that flag without being tagged. Sometimes we needed games with body contact rather than stealthy stalking. There were no routines, for our groups were always different.

Suddenly I was ahead of them all, rushing down the slopes of the ravine, letting out war whoops and deliberately falling in the loose scree and gravel. The energy picked up, and the group began crying out, not in panic but in the excitement of a new game, a new way to move through the secret dread of the wilderness. In seconds we were all at the bottom of the ravine, darting back and forth in a search for something, for nothing.

They were defused and ready to go on.

Most institutional care fails at the point when it cannot treat the patient as an individual. All mental disorders are so distinctive to the individual that no textbook cure is ever completely applicable. The Earth Adventures always left me incredulous that medical care is regulated, not to fit the doctor to each patient, but to ensure that all patients get the same kind of doctoring.

I had an image of a waterfall in my mind. Though I have never read anywhere of falling water being used as therapy for disturbed people, I had seen people in Haiti transported under the influence of falling water. On the

Nile both Cherif and I had felt the hypnotic pull of cataract waters rushing us onward. The human mind seemed to be highly receptive to the energy in the fall or flow of water. (I've since heard of studies that show a strong effect of negative ions in flowing water.) In New Jersey, we were heading for water. We were a few miles from the Water Gap, and I was ready to put my people on the river, the boats waiting at a prearranged point. For the rest of the morning we practiced in quiet water: basic strokes, capsizing and righting the canoes, and so on. After lunch I would line them up in a kind of LeMans racing start and get the canoe trip going with a bang.

When we burst out of the trees and into the full hot shower of sun on the rippling river waters, we must have looked like a bunch of crazed barbarians getting ready to invade Pennsylvania. By the time we got onto the water, the energy of the river had passed into us. The adventurers were as high as kites. I watched them from the lagging boat. Usually I paired a confident student with a timorous one, or some other combination of opposites. Barbara sat in front of me in my boat. The faces of the others were studies in release from many individual imprisonments that were just now beginning to lift.

The water trip was a gradual reintroduction to the straight world. Nearby were highways and houses and fears. But preserved—for a while, anyway—was that feeling of separation and uniqueness that the wilderness provides free. They knew that nobody could reach them easily on the river. We approached the rapids, a rather benign, gradually diminishing series of low waves stretching across the full width of the river and to a length of about a quarter mile. For a skilled canoeist it was nothing. But to these novices it was like a child's first roller-coaster ride. Adrenaline flowed. Barbara started crying.

"I'm not going down there," shouted JC, turning his boat sideways to the current and nearly upsetting it.

"We're all going to drown!" wailed Kate.

Monty calmed Susie, who sat between his knees at the bottom of their boat. "Everything is going to be all right," he told her. "We're going to make it."

In fact, if anybody chose to look over the side, the water was about three feet deep. But that did not matter. They tried to paddle upstream to avoid the rapids, but the current was just a little too strong for them, and they were carried helplessly down into the broken water. Real panic began at just about the time I took the lead. John Davenport paddled at our flank, ready to take to the water in a second.

"All right," I cried out, digging my paddle in deeply, "let's go it together. Follow me closely, but not too closely!"

Barbara took the lead from me. One of the supposedly "weak ones," she was now bowing her body almost double to get our canoe down into the rapids. The others saw this. JC did a double take.

Each of us was now alone with the responsibility of a paddle but also joined to the person behind or in front, and connected by the pull of the rapids to all the others. Anybody, it seemed, could drown here, but together we all could be safe. How many myths turn around the magic of water— as a grave, a mirror, a flood, a passageway, a resting place? We were exploring the race memory of the wilderness here, with no end to the possible effects of it.

Whenever challenged, the schizophrenics came through. One time a canoe overturned in the middle of the rapids; I saw legs going up in the air and heard the screams of the two "strong ones" in that canoe as they hit the water. I was about fifty feet away, plenty close enough for safety, but I dug deep to pull over to them. They stood up, sheepishly, in water that came to their waists. We had to stop at the end of the rapids so everybody could laugh out that scene.

After the rapids and the excitement we had a few miles of easygoing, tranquilizing water while the adrenaline completed its work. The adventurers did not know then how close they were to the end of their expedition. In a moment we would be ashore, and then into the vans and heading for the last camping place.

I spent more time figuring out how and where to end these adventures than on any other aspect of them. I needed seclusion for the inner wilderness charge, and a place that would draw the group close together for the communal effect. I wanted a waterfall, as in Haiti, and some element of danger. I must have walked a hundred miles trying to find the right spot.

When I did find it, there was a waterfall, all right, and also a deep, still pool. A high, overhanging rock jutted over the pool. There was no sense of the nearby river or highway. The surrounding rocks were covered with moss as they ran down into the pool waters. I called this place the Grotto. After getting rid of the canoes, and as we were slaving up through the woods to the plateau land that holds the Grotto, I regaled the group with tales of ancient Greece and Rome, where wood sprites made mischief in enchanted glades, and where fairy kings and queens played hob with other people's souls and psyches. By this time they all understood my schemes, and there was a sense of expectation.

I had discovered that there are many elements to the wilderness effect, many levels to its power. The mountains produce that grand, wild feeling of escape I had experienced in the Sierra with my father and elsewhere. The waterfall was pure electricity, leading to exaltation.

Barbara poised herself on the rock ledge, daring herself to jump. Kate discovered she could slide down the moss-covered rocks and straight into the pool. In moments we were a wild, abandoned group, the quiet woods ringing with hoots and cries and the crash of bodies hitting the waters of the Grotto.

Later, in the van and heading back in the twilight to Earth House, there was time to let the experience sink in. Some of it would stick and perhaps help guide the adventurers toward recovery. There can be no sudden changes in

Barbara wearing her new-found smile. DAVID SMITH.

disorders that have been entrenched for years. But it was a start. The following week all the adventurers in this group were wearing T-shirts, one of which they presented to me, bearing the hand-lettered declaration "Yes I Can."

I spent every Friday for six years, from 1973–79, at Earth House, unless I was out of the country. The multiday Earth Adventures were an opportunity for more extended contact with the "students." Since moving away from the Northeast I haven't been able to follow their futures closely. But they often write to me or call me, or I read of their fates, so I have a sense of what is happening for some of them. Rob, for instance, got a library job and became stable. Pete racketed around for a few years and then suddenly married and held a steady job. Juan killed himself in Venezuela, and Monty lost his life in an overdose of drugs in a hospital. Barbara, who had been a candidate for lobotomy, the survivor of two hundred shock treatments, made a complete turnaround, married, and now has a child. She wrote me, "I owe you for my smile." I almost cried, remembering a time when she couldn't walk and talk at the same time.

Barbara, like many other Earth Adventurers, had been in touch with the source. But how might she describe the experience? How might I trace her hesitant steps through the woods, the tiny suggestions of a return to a normal life? Despite my feeling of a close connection to the source, I still cannot confidently describe it or how it works.

Once when I was giving a videotape presentation of the Earth Adventure, the dean of the Chapel at Princeton University, Ernest Gordon, suddenly burst into applause and cried out, "That's the way it works! You've got it exactly!" Later I learned that during World War II, Gordon had been given up for dead in the notorious Japanese concentration camp whose inmates had built the famous bridge over the River Kwai. He had recovered, by himself, as a result of his own discovery of a source of hidden strength, the source I hoped to tap in each Earth Adventure.

After an adventure the group would return to Earth House. Everyone would be tired, and most of the participants would begin to feel the immensity of the world again, a great wall against them. They did not realize then that their wilderness experience had just begun. There had been self-discovery. Ahead, tantalizingly, was the possibility of normalcy, job, marriage, careers, total or partial cures.

One student who recovered completely wrote an article for his local newspaper in which he described his road back to health. The work of the source, the value of the Earth House experience, came together in a phrase that described it all—"that fragile, beautiful beginning."

Chapter 7

Pilgrimage to Shangri-La

The journey to Hunza from Islamabad, in Pakistan, usually takes about twenty-four hours by bus and jeep—that is, if the vehicles are not broken, or if there has not been an accident, or if the drivers have not decided to take a few days off. By plane it takes an hour, and then two-and-a-half hours in a jeep. I opted for the plane. But in that part of the world you simply do not opt. You make your decision and then you wait, for days if necessary. As a matter of fact I had waited for years to get to Hunza, that remote, mountain-ringed valley nestled under the Karakoram Range on Pakistan's northern frontier. There was never any hurry to get the traveler to Hunza. Nobody in Hunza really cared whether the traveler came or not.

Hunza is a once-independent Himalayan kingdom upon which James Hilton probably based his fictional Shangri-La, the locale for his novel *Lost Horizon*. Before the airplane and the Jeep it was practically inaccessible to all but the most determined travelers, and then only with risk. The people of Hunza were once notorious professional brigands.

My interest in Hunza was simple. I knew that the people there lived to great ages. There was apparently no mental illness and none of the degenerative diseases that preoccupy us—no tuberculosis, cancer, or heart disease. There was no crime, juvenile delinquency, drug problems, divorce, or, in my romantic view of the place, any unhappiness as we know it.

I was sure that the source of my own energy and athletic achievement would be readily accessible in everyday life in such a place. Hilton had dramatized the power of the source into everlasting life and beauty, which disappeared the moment one left Shangri-La. I knew the source was a universal phenomenon, but in the Western world, at least, it was not accessible to average people the way I felt that it must be in Hunza. It had been my dream for some years to go to Hunza, talk with the people there, live with them, test them, and compare my theories with their practices.

I tried on and off without success to get a visa for Hunza from 1969 (about the time of my Haitian run) until 1979, when I finally got there. I had wangled a tentative assignment from *Geo* magazine to write about Hunza and arrived in Islamabad with a professional photographer, Terry Moore. Still, it seemed that visas were not instantly available—at least not for an itinerant American who did not have a reason for visiting Hunza that any bureaucrat could understand.

Finally I went to the Pakistani Ministry of Information, where I managed to get an interview with the director, a man named Mohammed Saleem. As soon as I was able to make real human contact, everything became easier. Saleem was an ex-cricket player, worried about the paunch he had developed over his last few years behind a desk. I remarked casually that I was a physical fitness expert and had written a book on the subject. In a matter of moments we were lying on the floor of the director's office, our coats off and sleeves rolled up, performing a rigorous series of calisthenics.

"Would you consider it a terrible presumption, Mr. Smith," he asked, "if I asked you to prescribe for me a personal program of exercise?"

"Would you consider it a great imposition, Mr. Saleem," I replied, "if I asked you for a visa to Hunza?"

Within twenty hours I was on my way to Shangri-La. Before I left, Mohammed Saleem became highly interested in my project. "We are losing much of our ancient culture," he said. "We are imitating those parts of Western culture that give us immediate benefit. We forget that we have strengths and advantages, too, which should not be thrown away with our technological backwardness."

"I want to find a place that has escaped the major changes of this age," I said, "a place where the wisdom goes back further than yesterday afternoon and isn't based on a pill or a machine that will be obsolete tomorrow."

"Alas," said Saleem, "Jeeps have come to Hunza." But then he brightened. "Still, there are many old people and much resistance to change. They think we are barbarians down here in Islamabad. The pace of life is very slow there."

"The slower the better," I said. "I want to hear the mountains breathing."

"You will hear Jeep engines," replied Saleem.

Planes to Hunza fly so irregularly that the traveler might wait at Islamabad for ten days or more at a time while bad weather keeps the aircraft grounded, or, as I chose to believe, the pilots play gin rummy to decide whether they want to fly or not.

One day the clouds lifted somewhat, and I got my belongings onto a rather ancient propeller plane. I started down the aisle, and one of the flight attendants, who was smoking, told me where to sit. On one side of me was a Pakistani tax collector and on the other were two shepherds, who would spend most of the flight laughing to themselves about the American who thought he was flying to Shangri-La.

"You think you're going to paradise?" said the tax collector. "I hope you like hard work and cold water."

We flew north from Islamabad over terraced foothills into the Karakoram, a chaos of jagged peaks, vertical rock, and glacier snow. Before us towered Nanga Parbat, at nearly 27,000 feet; it is called the Naked Mountain because its slopes are too steep to hold snow. On the horizon, straddling the border with China, loomed K2, the second highest mountain in the world.

Before leaving Islamabad I had scribbled some notes in my journal. "Ah, Shangri-La," I had written. "Land of terraced mountain gardens and exquisite lotus pools. Land where youth and health are unaffected by the passage of time, and one is always hospitable to strangers, and crime is so rare as to be practically nonexistent. Land untouched and out of time with Western civilizations."

The pilot threaded his way through the snowy peaks. For long minutes we were well below their tops, and we seemed to be sinking steadily as they got higher and we headed toward Gilgit, an Asian frontier town that is the doorway to Hunza. At Gilgit I planned to make connections to Hunza and begin soaking up atmosphere. I knew intuitively that I would meet somebody who could direct me to my objective, as Mohammed Douda had welcomed me to Agadir after the Sahara Desert walk.

Through the center of Gilgit runs a two-mile-long bazaar, a place of apparent utter confusion, a zigzag of wooden shops whose proprietors hawk everything from aspirin to apricots at the tops of their voices. Some Hunzakuts, as they are called, had drifted into Gilgit and settled there, but most of the people I came across were Punjabi merchants, poor Afghan refugees, or Chinese workers on leave from the construction of the Karakoram Highway, the first road from China to the subcontinent through this part of the Himalaya that could accommodate wheeled vehicles.

In the lively confusion of the bazaar I knew I would find my man. It took about five minutes. He was an English-speaking merchant named Ghulam Mohammed Beg, a tall, swarthy, physically powerful man and a former polo champ. He was the leader of the Ismalic sect of the Muslim religion in Gilgit. We hit it off right away. Since I had studied Islam and had observed the thirty-day fast of Ramadan, we shared

Village in the Hunza Valley, with Rakaposhi at far left.
DAVID SMITH.

'

a

in

yo

be

kno

I left Aliabad and went on to Karimabad, where the Mir's palace is located. In centuries past the Hunzakuts waited astride Eastern caravan routes, making much of the trade between India and China extremely risky. When the arrival of the British in the nineteenth century brought an end to that life, the Hunzakuts quickly turned to cultivation of the land. In conforming to a new authority they did not lose either their spirit or their outlook. The source of their peculiar energies remained unchanged.

Nobody could be sure from whence the Hunzakuts came. Racially they were distinct from other peoples in this part of the world. Some writers have said that they are the descendants of officers who deserted from the army of Alexander the Great when he attempted to conquer India. According to other, more recent theories, they are a mixture of Indo-Aryan tribes who migrated from West Turkestan and then intermarried with indigenous mountain peoples.

I set out to absorb a sense of the place through a long and contemplative run. The air felt like chilled white wine. I filled my lungs. As I chugged along, a score of small boys tried to keep pace with me. They could run as fast as I could for a while, and when they finally stopped, they gave up hard, panting and gasping. It was obvious, as I dodged the rocks and skidded in the gravel, that despite its beauty this was a desperately hard place. I felt the presence of backbreaking work, and of a steel spine that ran through the landscape and held its occupants to the rigorous task of just surviving.

After an hour a lean, wiry young man joined me. He galloped alongside me, his robes flying in the breeze that was coming from the mountains.

"See our trees," he panted. "You like our trees?"

I said I liked his trees.

"We like trees," he said, "because they are hard to grow, yet they are useful and beautiful, and they are filled with the spirit. Are your trees filled with the spirit?"

Village in the Hunza Valley, with Rakaposhi at far left.
DAVID SMITH.

some common ground. We talked about the desert and the Gilgit mosque.

Mohammed Beg sold books on Islam and handicrafts from Hunza. His shop was an informal meeting place of resettled Hunzakuts. When we started talking about polo, a small crowd gathered. I had recently practiced my horsemanship, particularly tight, quick turns, in the hope of playing polo in Hunza, where the game was said to have originated.

"You've missed the finals in Gilgit," said Sirbaz Khan, one of the local polo heroes. He said the game was no longer played in Hunza.

"What!" I cried.

"It is a great tragedy," said Mohammed Beg. "Horses are on the way out. They must give way to the Jeep."

"Can I still ride a yak over the old road to Hunza?" I asked. This had been a dream when I first thought about visiting Hunza.

My friend shook his head no. "The yaks are in the cooler, high country," he told me. "You can travel by Jeep on the new KKH in three hours."

"KKH?"

"The Karakoram Highway, out of China."

Though the names conjured the romance and history of the place, I suddenly saw Jeeps bouncing through my vision of an unspoiled landscape.

The government Jeep left for Hunza in the midafternoon. With me rode Riaz Ahmed Khan, a thirty-year-old official of the Pakistan Tourism Development Corporation; he was there to help me get started.

"You will find your atmosphere, all right; I promise you that," he kept saying. "There is no place of greater peace on earth than the remote district of Hunza."

As he spoke, we were rushing along a boulder-strewn road at seventy to eighty miles an hour, the driver's foot flat to the floorboards and the whole vehicle screaming with the stress of being so savagely overdriven. It was a relief to come to a checkpoint.

"My passport number?"

A wave of hands and big, toothy smiles.

"A number, any number; it is of no importance."

After Gilgit the landscape turned mostly barren. The Hunza River cut through the rock; on either side lay deserts of snow and ice and scrambled stones. Then suddenly I saw the face of Mount Rakaposhi, the guardian of the Hunza Valley. The sudden appearance of the valley, seen through the shuddering windshield of the Jeep, was pure storybook. But I was so busy hanging on to the panic bars and praying for survival that I could hardly look at it. Finally, in a scream of brakes and a cloud of dust, we came to a halt.

All at once, it seemed, I found myself sitting in a chair on the well-kept lawn of a traditional Hunza house composed of mud, bricks, and stones. It was in the village of Aliabad at the home of Yaoob Khan, Riaz's father. I had arranged a meeting here with a man named Shreen Khan, who, at the age of 105, had just stopped his work of feeding the chickens and goats every day. He now moved around his garden with the aid of a sawn-off polo mallet. He wore a trim, white goatee, and his weather-beaten face looked like that of a seventy-year-old. We sat together listening to Yaoob play the sitar.

"I was about twenty when the British came in," said Shreen Khan.

"When was that?" I asked.

"That would have been 1891," he replied.

A faint smell of honeysuckle filled my nostrils. Before me lay the Hunza River, with Mount Rakaposhi's majestic bulk rising to 25,550 feet behind it. Green fields and orchards rose in terraces, some nearly perpendicular, to the steep slopes of the mountain houses nestled among poplars and apricot trees and looking like refugees from reality. Higher up the mountain stood a massive fortress, built about five

Shreen Khan. DAVID SMITH.

hundred years ago as a gesture of good will by the neighboring kingdom of Ladakh, or "Little Tibet." Beyond that were glaciers and 24,000-foot snowy peaks. I had stepped into a magic kingdom. It was Shangri-La.

When there is accord between man and nature, between self and place, then there is contact with the source. The individual is projected into the place that he or she idealizes. Here in Hunza I could feel the emptiness of the desert, the peace of the Nile, the lack of all external pressure. I sat in paradise, feeling the power of the source all around me.

I drank tea with the locals. Mohammed Shafa, a teacher at a girls' school talked eloquently in English. Others surrounding us interjected comments. It was a cram course of learning.

"This source, this power that you talk about; a lot of it you will feel from those," said Shafa, inclining his head toward the distant but starkly visible Himalayas. "We are people of the mountains, captives of them, perhaps, and we cannot move here without feeling their influence on us."

I asked for some of their history.

"Our forefathers tell us Ganesh was the first village here, then Baltit and Altit. The people of these villages needed someone to settle their differences, so they brought in an outsider. That was the Mir. But he is not one of us."

"How long ago was that?" I asked.

"Four or five hundred years."

"How long does it take to become one of you?" I asked, but nobody cracked a smile.

"What it takes to become a Hunzakut," Shafa replied, "is the ability to look at a pile of boulders, gravel, and sand, and instead of feeling defeat and despair, to see fertile soil in that place and then flourishing crops. To be a Hunzakut you must have this great imagination to see what seems to be impossible."

"You have to have faith?" I asked.

"You have to have an accommodation with what is not known," he answered.

I left Aliabad and went on to Karimabad, where the Mir's palace is located. In centuries past the Hunzakuts waited astride Eastern caravan routes, making much of the trade between India and China extremely risky. When the arrival of the British in the nineteenth century brought an end to that life, the Hunzakuts quickly turned to cultivation of the land. In conforming to a new authority they did not lose either their spirit or their outlook. The source of their peculiar energies remained unchanged.

Nobody could be sure from whence the Hunzakuts came. Racially they were distinct from other peoples in this part of the world. Some writers have said that they are the descendants of officers who deserted from the army of Alexander the Great when he attempted to conquer India. According to other, more recent theories, they are a mixture of Indo-Aryan tribes who migrated from West Turkestan and then intermarried with indigenous mountain peoples.

I set out to absorb a sense of the place through a long and contemplative run. The air felt like chilled white wine. I filled my lungs. As I chugged along, a score of small boys tried to keep pace with me. They could run as fast as I could for a while, and when they finally stopped, they gave up hard, panting and gasping. It was obvious, as I dodged the rocks and skidded in the gravel, that despite its beauty this was a desperately hard place. I felt the presence of back-breaking work, and of a steel spine that ran through the landscape and held its occupants to the rigorous task of just surviving.

After an hour a lean, wiry young man joined me. He galloped alongside me, his robes flying in the breeze that was coming from the mountains.

"See our trees," he panted. "You like our trees?"

I said I liked his trees.

"We like trees," he said, "because they are hard to grow, yet they are useful and beautiful, and they are filled with the spirit. Are your trees filled with the spirit?"

I said that our trees were filled with the spirit, but not many people knew this.

"Once," he said, "my father's poplar tree, which grew near the border of his neighbor's property, became a problem. The neighbor said it was too close, and it made shade he did not want, and its roots were stealing his fertility by extending across the boundary line of the properties. It was work for the Mir. But we did not have a Mir. You understand?"

I knew that the Mir had been the absolute ruler of the Hunzakuts. Local disputes were settled by village chiefs, but their decisions could be appealed to the Mir's council. The British encouraged the Mirs but bent them to British rules. Then, under Pakistani rule, the powers of the Mir were deemed to be too great, and the government ostensibly retired the last of them in 1974.

Yet there was still a Mir's palace at Karimabad, and it was occupied by Gazenfra Khan, the son of the late Mir. Among the Hunzakuts at least, he seemed to have all the power and responsibility of a Mir. He kept Hunza's official guest-book, which, when I signed it, showed me the signatures of Lowell Thomas (1917), Chou Enlai (1966), and U.S. Senator Charles Percy (1970s).

The value of the Mir and his council was that he was in touch with the people and rocks and sand and gravel of this place. The new district courts, established in larger towns by a government a thousand miles away, did not have the sensitivity of the old system.

"The local council said to uproot the tree," the wiry young man said, "because it was leaching the neighbor's land."

"Yes," I said.

"But the higher court said to leave the tree," the young man continued.

"Yes," I said. "Was that not right?"

"Perhaps it was," said the young man.

"Then what is this story all about?"

"The neighbor diverted my father's water supply," the young man replied.

"What happened to the tree?" I asked.

"Oh, the tree," said the young man, "that was not important."

Eventually I outran him. I backtracked easily through the center of Hunza, past the capital in Karimabad, the Mir's guest house, palace, and government house comprising Karimabad in its totality. I pushed along the dusty, dung-strewn road (the dung would soon be picked up; since the soil is so impoverished, every available fertilizer is used, including human sewage) and headed up toward the fort at Baltit, the former capital. The mountains were as blue as a towering sea. In about an hour I had traversed the most heavily inhabited main part of the valley and had reached the Karakoram Highway.

The highway started near Islamabad, in the Indus Valley, and cut through the Karakoram Range via Hunza to reach into Sinkiang Province in southwestern China. I had been told that its construction had been pushed out of China with ruthless determination, and that one man had died for every mile of its five-hundred-mile length. Almost at once I passed a monument built by the Chinese for some of the "martyrs" who had died building the road. A short time later I came across a rock the size of a pickup truck lying in the middle of the road, evidence of the frequent rockslides throughout this mountainous terrain. Behind it some Pakistani soldiers were shoveling gravel debris off the road.

Beyond, the old Hunza road snaked breathtakingly up into a wall of rock. This was the old suicide pass, which had claimed hundreds of vehicles from the time the first Jeep arrived in Hunza in 1948. In the old days the Mir was fond of saying, "There are only perfect drivers in Hunza." The wreckage of smashed vehicles, lying far down in the valley, bespoke a fearful carnage.

In climbing two thousand feet along this road, I began to feel the shortage of oxygen; it made my limbs tingle and my breath drive deeper into my lungs. But oddly, although I was short of breath, my limbs were in terrific shape, and I felt I could run for another couple of hours if I could keep my breath. Also, because I had not studied a map, I had no real idea of where I was, or where the road led, or if it was designated off-limits by the military, or how far I was from the Chinese border. Actually, as I found later, the border was about seventy miles distant and there wasn't any map.

About halfway through the second hour I heard an engine behind me, and I moved over to the roadside to give the driver plenty of room to pass. Pedestrians have no rights in this new Jeep age of the Karakoram, and I had no desire to become a topic of tea-time discussions concerning the weekly road mortalities. But at once a brilliantly colored Jeep, covered with decals of mountain scenes and religious signs, and equipped with oversized sun visors and tires, flags, pennants, extra fuel tanks, thick carpeting, and quadruple air horns mounted on its hood, pulled ahead of me, braked, and then slowed to a stop in my path. It was filled with grinning Hunzakuts.

Slowly, and with great and measured dignity, a man got out of the passenger side. He nodded to me, carefully smoothed his double-breasted English suit, and adjusted his pearl gray fedora. He looked like someone out of a James Cagney movie of the thirties.

"My name is Altaf Hussain," the man announced formally, "and the telling is that you make swimming."

I shook his hand and said that I was pleased to meet him.

"I swim, too," he said, "and challenge therefore, you, to contest."

"A race?"

"We swim across river," he said.

Everybody in the Jeep laughed.

"I sorry," he added, "I cannot speak."

He meant English, but I could not tell if he was serious.

"If there is a challenge," I replied, "we must race for something."

"Something?"

"A prize," I said. "Let's say a yak."

Altaf turned to the Jeep. "I am liking this man."

He faced me again. "As you make it," he said, giving that sideways inclination of his head that is Asia's gesture of agreement, regret, approval.

The men in the Jeep cried out, "Altaf will win!"

One man said, "He taught many of us how to swim."

I said, "I have to tell you that I am a very good swimmer. I didn't come to Hunza just to steal someone's yak."

They all grinned.

Altaf drew himself up and beat his fists on his chest. Then he cried out, "I am best swimmer at village. I am best swimmer by all Hunza. I am best swimmer in northern provinces. I am Altaf!"

That seemed to clinch it, although I was already regretting my impulse to get into a contest as a means of learning about the place and its people.

I ran toward the setting sun. Then suddenly I cut off the KKH, leaving Altaf and his Jeep companions to their own affairs, and sprinted up a tree-lined track, along which farmers, many of them old and smiling, were moving back toward home at the end of their dawn-till-dusk working day in the "fields." Women carrying large bundles on their backs scurried out of my way. Some merely turned their heads or draped a colorful scarf over their faces after they'd taken a good look at me. I was feeling really good—lean and fit and buoyant. The air was marvelous despite the dust, and I began to understand why all these people had such brilliant lights in their eyes. They looked the way I felt. Everywhere, I could see where they had piled rocks out of the way to make the path clear, to remove rockslides that come down the mountainsides constantly. I ran to keep fit, but they did this kind of thing every day, every month, and every year of their lives. No wonder they lived to be more than a hundred. By the time Karimabad came into view again it was twilight, and the light was fading fast. I had been running for two-and-a-half hours. To my astonishment there were lights on in the town. The power had been off for six months, and it was a real shock for everybody on the road to see the village lit with electricity. As I puffed along, I also began to see flaming torches appear on the roofs of all the houses. It was the birthday of Ali, the son-in-law of the prophet Mohammed. Beyond Hunza I could see fires shining from about two thousand feet above the line of cultivation. Shepherds were getting into the spirit, even though they could not leave their flocks to join the celebration in the valley.

That night I worked my way through the village, getting to know people and testing their vital signs. I had brought a few basic biofeedback instruments with me. I wanted to compare the young and the old and measure their vitality against mine. I used a galvanic-skin-response instrument for measuring skin perspiration triggered by the nerves. The GSR is the familiar lie-detector, and I wondered whether it could be used to confirm the Hunzakuts' claimed ages. Apparently their longevity had become so renowned that they might tell a stranger they were older than was really the case, if they thought that was what the stranger wanted to hear. I also had a spironometer, which measured vital capacity, or the amount of oxygen used by the lungs. A blood pressure gauge tested the state of the vascular wall. The pressure exerted by the blood upon the walls of the blood vessels varied with the muscular efficiency of the heart, the blood volume and viscosity, and the age and health of the individual. I also tested heart rates and reflexes.

The astonishing thing about the Hunzakuts, I found, was that they were human beings without anxiety. Whenever I was among them I felt no negative energy at all. Each Hunzakut sat before me, face relaxed and eyes clear and unquestioning, as he or she accepted my explanation that I was testing the force—the source—of their lives, which were a mystery to me. They watched as my strange machines were unpacked and attached to them, but there was simply no apprehension. After a while I understood why. They were not anxious because nothing I could do would ever shake them. This quality made the issue of their truthfulness about their ages rather moot.

"You are nervous man," one Hunzakut told me.

I felt as calm as I had ever been. But it was a matter of degree. The man looked at me with a gaze of such total serenity that I did, indeed, feel "nervous" in comparison with him.

As I got to know the Hunzakuts, talking to them, interviewing them, and testing them, I began to sense how powerfully the mountains figured in their lives. Person after person talked about "going up" into the mountains, where many of them worked. "Of course, it is better in the mountains," I was told. The best hunting was in the mountains. And in bygone days the best robberies. They accepted the mountains, and had for hundreds of years, as harsh modulators of their lives.

I met seventy-seven-year-old Laiman Shah, a blue-eyed patriarch who was known for having planted 100,000 poplar trees in Hunza, a feat more or less comparable to a resident of Manhattan singlehandedly returning his island to deep forest. He wore a heavy overcoat and a striking pair of high, soft leather boots. I never saw him, at other times, without a heavy load of materials. He was, like his camels of years past, a voluntary beast of burden.

"Fifty years ago," Laiman Shah said calmly, and contentedly in the memory of it, "I was a camel driver working the road to Sinkiang."

That is to say, he had traversed the death-ridden old road into China, which was so dangerous that hundreds of camels were lost every year to rockslides, avalanches, and missteps. He liked the work for the physical connection it gave him with place, and because all the men on the road were forged out of the same dangers.

I also interviewed Zoltan Beg, an eighty-six-year-old man who had one of the highest farms in the mountains. Several times each week he walked from his farm to Aliabad and back, a five-mile roundtrip involving a 4,000-foot altitude change.

"It is true," he said, "that there is less old age today than there was."

"How do you measure this?" I asked.

He replied, "When my father reached 100, he had twenty friends the same age. Today I have only six friends who are beyond ninety."

Obviously an uncheckable statistic, but something more than an old man's musings.

Each Hunzakut, it seemed to me, bore a distinct imprint from the mountain world in which he or she lived. There were no "masses" in Hunza, only hundreds of individuals, each with a different story. That was striking.

"You should meet Ali Murad," various people said. They felt that he represented the kind of spirit I was looking for: an elderly, active man who personified the notion—my notion, rather—of Shangri-La. Eventually this meeting was arranged.

I waited for Ali Murad in the house of Qudratulla Beg, one of the respected elders of Baltit, who was writing a book on the history of Hunza. His authorship was at three levels: researching the letters exchanged between the Mirs, kings, and other heads of state; writing; and intense discussions with almost everybody about what he had written. He had been at work on this project for sixty years. It was obvious that completion of the book would be a tragedy for him. We were drinking salted tea (my first and last experience

Ali Murad (Juno), "the old man of Baltit." DAVID SMITH.

with that very strange drink) on a balcony overlooking the household's courtyard, a place constantly swarming with activity.

Suddenly a kind of whirlwind bounded into the courtyard. He was wiry, with brilliant orange hair, henna-dyed in one of the habits of Hunza. He stood there, his head cocked to one side, making some kind of joke to the women who swarmed around him, laughing. Then he dashed up the stairs toward the balcony.

"This is Ali Murad, the old man of Baltit," said my host.

"We call him by his nickname, Juno, which means 'darling.' "

In an instant my right hand was clamped in Juno's fist and his sparkling eyes were appraising me, running up and down my body and looking deeply into my eyes, with a vast question in them.

"Are you alive?" they seemed to be asking. "Will I be able to talk to this man from a distant place, this man who wants to test my blood and my skin, and find out why I am 102 years of age?"

His appraisal completed, he immediately launched into a voluble account of his life, using quick, sharp gestures, constantly adjusting his body in the chair. It was true, he said, that something in the mountains belonged to the people of Hunza. He thought it was the spirit of the Almighty. "It is a power that lives in the place."

Any Hunzakut could feel this spirit, even in the foothills, and when you got far back in the mountains, "around Gilgit," it was very powerful indeed. "It makes you very strong. It's the water!" He laughed.

But he did not think that it had anything to do with his longevity, or the long lives of any other Hunza residents.

"Longevity is a very simple matter," he said. "It comes about because of good plain food, good mountain water, and a great deal of hard work." I was surprised to discover that although he was on the Council of Elders of Hunza, he was still a farmer and did quite a bit of work on his own land.

When I asked him whether there was any fear in Hunza, he laughed. There was fear everywhere. Fear was a friend. It comes "and gives us energy to climb, and to work, when we are in doubt."

Juno was saying, in effect, that fear was like the mountain itself—a friend if you embraced it but a deadly enemy if you were frightened of fear itself.

"It is not the conquest of fear that is important," he said, laughing again. "It is the putting of fear to work."

In Aeschylus's *Orestia*, the goddess Athena refuses Orestes' demand that the Furies be expelled from Athens forever. Out of the city, she warned, the Furies would be redoubled enemies at Athens. Inside the city their enormous energies might be put to work for the benefit of the entire community. Her plan worked. Now, hearing Juno's words, I felt I was in touch with classical times, as if two thousand years of wisdom had been compressed into a few sentences.

When I tested Juno's vital signs, I found a blood pressure of 120/60, or about the same as that of a twenty-year-old Western man, and a strong pulse of 60, very slow and deep.

"I hope you find what you are looking for," he said, crushing my hand again. Then he bounded down the stairs and across the courtyard to his next meeting of the Council of Elders.

Unfortunately there was only one Juno, and there were many Jeeps. But undoubtedly the ubiquitous Jeep made the life of modern Hunza possible. It carried produce, tugged heavy loads, and transported highway-repair workers to distant parts of the valley. It also brought in sick sheep and raced down the bumpy highways, dust boiling from its wheels, to rescue the human injured and sick. It was a completely Western tool of progress, and its benefits could not be disputed or its convenience discounted.

During my testing and interviewing Altaf Hussain kept chasing after me—not two or three times but like a gnat biting a mountain sheep again and again.

"Are you ready?" he cried, his Jeep skidding to a halt under my window.

"Are you ready?" he shouted from the courtyard, the sound of his Jeep engine in the lane outside.

I saw Altaf eventually as Jeepman. The village started calling our arrangement "The Challenge," viewing it as the continuing drama of a man who went everywhere in a Jeep, often alongside another man who went everywhere in running shoes and a T-shirt that said "Save the Whales."

"Let us turn The Challenge into a festival," said Ghulam Mohammed Beg, who had come from Gilgit on a short visit. "We will bring down a yak from the high country and have the winner ride up the mountainside. We will get musicians from Mominabad and slaughter a goat. The loser pays for everything." Then he had a thought. "We could have the race in the large pool at Altit."

"Why?" I asked.

"Because it is safer," he replied.

"And Altaf will win in the river," chimed in Mohammed Shafa.

I hesitated. I did not relish the dangers of extreme cold. I had never swum in a freezing Himalayan river before, and I certainly had never competed through towering rapids. The pool, which was actually a holding tank for an irrigation system, was described to me as challenging; still, the river beckoned.

"In the last swim of the river," warned Zefrilla Khan of Baltit as I was taking his blood pressure, "four died."

I took a Jeep to Altit, more to think things over than to see the pool; but even before I reached my destination, I decided that it would have to be the river or nothing. Swimming in the pool seemed a bit like taking a Jeep everywhere. I figured there was hardly any chance of Altaf beating me in the pool. The point of our contest, it seemed to me, was to test the tough mountain man, in his own environment, against the visitor who sought to find out how he might fit into this unique world.

"Are you ready?" cried Altaf Hassain when I returned.

"The river," I said. "Tomorrow."

"I like this man," he said to his Jeep companions.

In the morning I got up at dawn. It was a brilliant, sunny day, ideal for any kind of challenge. I ran to the postbox nailed to a tree to mail a card to my parents, and then

I took a cold shower to make me respect the river. Exhilaration. Acclimation. The tailor sent over my swimsuit, repaired beautifully. The band arrived to play our music. A procession began forming in Karimabad to accompany me down to the river. Afrazullah Beg, a former Pakistani Army officer from Hyderabad, was concerned about the possibility of me drowning and of Hunza's liability. "Drowning is very common in the river," he said. "Last year, in the race near Gilgit, eighteen started and four drowned. Would you perhaps reconsider?"

I just smiled.

"You have swum the mighty Colorado, of course?" he went on, seeking some kind of reassurance.

I said I had not but added, "I have swum in many strange places."

"Oh," he said, and tried to leave it at that. But he could not, and a few minutes later he came running after me in the procession and handed me a slip of paper. It read:

UNDERTAKING

AT MY SWEET WILL, I VENTURE TO CROSS RIVER HUNZA WITH MR. ALTAF HUSSAIN OF VILLAGE GANESH. IN CASE OF CASUALTY (DROWNING), NONE ELSE BUT I MYSELF WILL BE FULLY RESPONSIBLE FOR THE LOSS OF MY LIFE. I HEREBY SIGN.

DAVID SMITH & TWO WITNESSES

Altaf came rushing up in his Jeep. It was decided that Afrazullah Beg would act as the referee, and at once he wanted to know which section of the river we planned to swim. The Hunza River separates Hunza from the neighboring state of Nagar. I said that we should start on the Nagar side of the river, upstream from a suspension bridge over the rapids there, taking care not to get near the cable hanging from the old bridge. This way we would finish on the Hunza side.

"No, no!" cried Altaf. "We swim below bridge, below rapids, from Hunza across to Nagar."

I agreed for the moment to swim Altaf's route. "But we've got to get out of the water before the next set of rapids farther downriver," I said, "or it's curtains for both of us."

"Curtains?"

I made a motion of cutting my own throat. Everybody laughed.

We decided to check out the river from the bridge. From there the flow of the current was visible enough, snaking through a dozen twists and turns, but there was no way of calculating the sizes of the rocks in the rapids. We decided to make the final decision from the river itself.

By this time crowds of people were watching. Scores were crammed onto the bridge for a true grandstand position. Hundreds stood watching from the mountainside, where they could get a view of the entire swim. Many others crowded along the fringes of the village of Ganesh, where high ground gave them a good vantage.

Once Altaf and I got down to the level of the river for a closer look, he changed his tune. We decided to start from a black, sandy beach well above the bridge. Then I lost touch with Altaf in the milling crowds and didn't see him for several minutes. Suddenly he appeared, a solitary figure waiting on the opposite bank. There was a cheer, and I had this flash: mountain man waiting confidently for city man.

But to reach him I had to traverse quite a bit of country. I began climbing the mountain, sliding, slipping, holding onto rocks to stop my fall. By the time I reached the KKH, I felt winded. I raced over the bridge, past the white lions sitting on every other post, and then climbed down the rocks to the beach. I was nearly out of breath, but this was no time to stop. I dived in, and the icy water, which looked like swirling gray graphite, knocked the rest of the breath right out of me so that I felt compressed, crushed by it. The water temperature was 39 degrees Fahrenheit. When I came up out of the water, my face and the top of my head flaming

Altaf (left) and David enter the Hunza River to begin their race. **PETER TURJE.**

with the cold, I fell to my knees on the beach. Altaf raised his arms. There came an immediate roar from the crowd. Altaf stood proudly, legs apart.

I took my place, upriver from Altaf. After I nodded that I was ready, the referee yelled, "One, two, three, go!"

We ran to the icy river, our feet sinking into the soft glacial sand. Altaf plunged in just ahead of me, and immediately I knew I had misjudged him. I put everything into my first sprint, but he drew ahead. Excitement overcame the feeling of being cold. Distantly I heard shouts.

With my head down I continued to sprint, trying to make up the loss. But Altaf stayed ahead. By the time we reached the rapids we were battling shoulder to shoulder. I thought I was a master of rough water, which was what made me a good marathon swimmer in the open sea. But Altaf was strong. I couldn't shake him. Each of us was in a position to crack the other in the head with a fist or an elbow. But he was a gentleman. The rapids got worse, and we bobbed and roller-coastered over rocks as if we were stuck together.

I pulled up my head for a second to get a better look ahead. We had only reached the center of the current, and in order to complete the course and reach the other bank, we simply had to swim through it, and quickly now or else we would be swept on downriver and into the second, more dangerous rush of rapids.

With my head down again I strove to bite into the whipping current. It was the craziest race I had ever swum. All at once I felt Altaf weakening, and I had a sudden rush of concern. I hoped he could make it through the current before the next rapids. I got into it, really hard, and my guts gave a surge: I was pouring it on like a madman. Through the spume I saw Altaf's agonized face, his brown arm upflung as he, too, cut into the racing water.

Suddenly the bite of the current diminished, as if I were being released from a lethal bondage. I was into a few feet of slower-moving water; then sand and rock were under my palms, and I was staggering in the shallows. I looked back— Altaf was still battling the current. One of his friends was running into the river, gesticulating, but he was losing Altaf by a hundred feet. I could hear the rapids roaring.

But then I saw what made Altaf the champion swimmer of the northern provinces, of all Pakistan, perhaps. He poured it on, cutting into the current. Abruptly he was free of it. He was safe. I found myself collapsing, utterly exhausted, on Shafa's shoulder.

Shafa cried out, "No more swimming here for Mr. David!" There were tears in his eyes. "Mr. David, you are brave men. Please, you both never swim this terrible river again. We entreat you!"

The spectators were raising all kinds of noise as Altaf and I staggered up to each other and shook hands, then put our arms over each other's shoulders and lurched up toward the waiting crowd.

After congratulating both of us, Afrazullah Beg made a

speech. Then he presented me with a garland of flowers and a certificate, which read:

CERTIFICATE

I AM PLEASED TO ANNOUNCE TO EVERYONE AROUND ON THE BANK OF RIVER HUNZA THAT MR. DAVID SMITH CROSSED THE RIVER MAGNIFICENTLY WITH MR. ALTAF HUSSAIN TODAY, THE 16TH OF JUNE, 1979, AT 1600 HOURS. IN THE CONTEST, MR. DAVID STANDS FIRST AND STANDS AT THE VICTORY TABLE. I WISH HIM GOOD-LUCK AND GOD SPEED HIM.

Afrazullah Beg
Ex-Junior Commissioned Officer
Pakarmy of Hunza

I jumped on the back of the scrawny yak for the ceremonial ride up the mountainside. A boy kicked the yak in the flanks. The animal sprinted forward, and my head snapped back sharply. The crowd let out a roar. It was very festive as we returned to Karimabad, the music following us. Hundreds of people wanted to shake my hand. I felt like a hero in a real-life fantasyland.

"You never do this again," people kept saying with genuine concern, smiling and shaking their heads. It had been a marvelous and exciting contest, but the fate of the men was more important to them than being entertained. I thought of the stadium crowds of my youth. I did not quite know what the difference was at that moment, but it seemed a profound one.

A dance began in front of the resthouse. Traditionally the winner dances first. I did a few steps, hops, and a circling motion, but then Shafa taught me how to do it. Then it was Altaf's turn. Then anybody who got the urge danced.

"Tomorrow," shouted Altaf, "I throw gigantic feast!"

Cheers.

One man danced on and on, dressed like a monster in a homemade costume. The three-piece band—a reeded flute and two drums—played for hours.

In the distance I could see the Karakoram Range darkening with the purple shadows of evening. I felt I had truly found Shangri-La. I was content.

They wanted me to make a speech, and there were cheers and then a hush when I stood up. That hush, a thousand faces expectant before me.

No sound of Jeep engines.

Chapter 8

Blackwater

Jeri Carlson was fed up with herself. Grossly overweight for most of her life, she had had her first date (a blind date at that) at 23. Now she was determined to take action. The stoop-shouldered insurance agent, John Dolger, was making an attempt to escape from a perpetual low-grade depression. Two months after the death of her husband, Madeline Smith remained hurt and confused and suffered almost unbearable feelings of loss and abandonment. She hoped to clear up the mental and emotional cobwebs with action.

A radio announcer, Victor Anselm—paunchy, chain-smoking, a funny guy—was determined to change his life around completely; his goal was to drop the paunch and stop drinking and smoking in thirty days. George Sutherland, a dentist, had been warned that his hypertension and eating habits would one day give him medical problems. He wanted to act now.

The exemplar of the group, though, was a diffident, warm, twenty-six-year-old pharmacist's assistant, Janet McCluskey, who had made a halfhearted suicide attempt, was ashamed of herself, and wanted to "turn my life around, somehow, in some way I can't figure out at the moment."

To me Janet epitomized the great national purposiveness of running, swimming, trekking, meditating, studying Oriental religions, and participating in any number of other self-improvement activities that began sweeping the country in the 1970s. This was 1980; I had come a long way from my first swim at the Golden Gate, and it seemed like the rest of America was starting to catch up.

We were standing under the pine trees of a Florida state park, on the threshold of a new sort of adventure. This time, however, not just David Smith but the entire group was on public view. Cameras from the local television station were focused on us: a group of runners.

The times were changing rapidly. The number of people in the United States who ran regularly was estimated at 25 million. In fact, nearly half of all the shoes sold every year were running shoes. I was moving along with the times. I had come home in a gradual way from my overseas wanderings as I passed through my thirties. I was married, with two children, and settled in Pensacola, Florida. I was in school again, studying modern communications at the University of West Florida, and spent most of my free time ranging the north Florida countryside to find places to kayak and run, secluded wilderness areas where nature could be experienced in my way.

Now it was my plan to put together my university studies and my experiences in search of the source. Television influenced the minds and bodies of millions. It was the artificial equivalent of the source I had discovered in wild places. It created heroes and villains, attitudes and desires. Above all it was a sports medium. It portrayed athletic enterprise so thrillingly that watching televised sports often proved more exciting than actually attending the event itself. I believed that television had stimulated millions to get into good physical shape, but it also had created an immense audience of utterly passive sports watchers.

The local station had become interested in my studies

of television as they related to my experiences and theories about the healing wilderness. They asked me if I would be willing to help them develop a program on the subject. Not only would I be willing to help, I would be ready to produce it. And so began the Blackwater Adventure Run.

The idea was to take a group of out-of-shape, very ordinary people and ask them to make a substantial commitment of time and effort to improve their physical condition and their lives overall. We would train them to run a kind of mini-marathon, a ten-mile run that I called a "wilderness obstacle course." This was designed to combine the wilderness effect, the stress of training, the challenge of personal change, and the transcendence of the healing journey.

I wanted the event and the participants to be in sharp contrast to the usual television fare of sports spectaculars. There would be no athletic hype; the run would not be staged as a competition. My own experiences of kayaking the Nile and swimming the Hunza River, of dealing with drug addicts and schizophrenics, centered on turning competition into an interior challenge, and this was my intent for the Blackwater Adventure Run. It would be an opportunity for ordinary people to find out that they were actually extraordinary.

These Blackwater people were not dropouts, and they had not thrown themselves on the mercy of society. They were functioning in the world, but they were in trouble of one kind or another. Part of their difficulty was the ailment of our century: that unfocused, helpless feeling of not being in charge. First I had to make them understand that the running alone would not change them or make them feel better. I emphasized the necessity of clearing the mind.

"We are aiming for a state of perfect accord between you and your surroundings, a connection with the flow of energy that I call the source. To reach it we are going to do as much talking as running, at first."

But, I pointed out, there would be problems. All of them must feel stress. But it must not be too severe, or they would be set back farther from the goal than before.

"You must be confident that you'll reach the source," I said, "and not become overanxious. The harder you pursue the state, the more elusive it will become. When we go into the wilderness, you'll need to risk but not wreck yourselves. We stagnate without enough challenge, but too much challenge cripples. We are looking for a middle ground. The wilderness stimulates the senses; yet a great calmness prevails there. You'll swell into this calmness and find yourself. Once you've become accustomed to it, you'll be able to see it clearly. Then it will give you what you want. You'll feel the electric charge that comes from the universe."

At the start of the program the participants shared their experiences in talk sessions, which became an essential part of the Blackwater experience. As the group became comfortable with one another, the intimacy grew, allowing each person to confess his or her feelings in a circle of safety.

Jeri Carlson: "I've been so ashamed of myself."

Madeline Smith: "Was it love I felt for him or just a terrible dependency?"

John Dolger's depression acquired a different quality when it was bounced off Victor Anselm's funny stories, his irrepressible good humor. George Sutherland emphasized that dentistry had taught him health was everything, and it started with healthy teeth and gums. Then he laughed at himself, saying, "I've really got to practice what I preach."

Janet McCluskey's suicide attempt took on another dimension when she talked about it, at first hesitantly. She began to see it as a device to get the attention of her overbearing father.

We often ran with one person's feelings in the air. Our cohesiveness as a group grew stronger. As we swung into more rigorous training, though, each participant got daily recharges of separateness in the parklands through which we would make our run.

"Listen to the silence," I said. "Feel the animals in the woods, the worms in the grasses. Imagine yourself a tree, your blood as sap."

Jeri Carlson lost eight pounds the first week. The dentist remained doubtful, but "I look forward to the talks." Carefully, we had no long-range goals. Each person aimed at doing one small thing on the following day.

We ran every day of the training. We came through the woods in a loose group—all together, yet each experiencing separate difficulties. We could often imagine what was in the others' minds. "I'm not going to make this," John Dolger said to himself. "I mean, what's the purpose? I'm still depressed." Victor Anselm was groaning. "I can't do it," he said, as his tobacco-choked lungs gave out on him. Janet McCluskey was feeling terrific: "I can't believe how centered I'm starting to feel." We plunged down Apache Canyon. I had given colorful names to points throughout the Blackwater so they would stick in the minds of the participants.

I ran along with them. I said nothing when I saw them in the grip of the challenge. They were doing things none of them had ever done before—taking risks, accepting challenges, and moving beyond their pain. George had to overcome his fear of a heart attack. Janet discovered that she could do anything the others could do. Jeri lost twenty more pounds after she discovered that weight loss was rapidly reducing the pains in her legs.

For each of them this was high-risk country, the same as for the athlete jumping out of a plane with his chute banging on his back. The adrenaline flowed for the suddenly unsedentary as it did for the hang-glider pilot going off El Capitan. There was a sense, too, of imminent discovery as each person advanced into territory that was new and often quite frightening.

"Where does this *extra* energy come from?" asked Madeline Smith. A familiar question to me, but giving them *my* answer was not the point.

For each of them the stress and the pain were as great as could be borne, yet it would be nothing much to an ath-

Jeri Carlson near the end of training. BILL HINTON.

lete. These nonathletes might drop out before they began
sweating, but they were coming alive. Bodies hurled to the
ground—"I can't do it!"—but there was a triumphant note
in there, a realization that they *were* doing it, and they knew
it even as they hit the dirt.

We pounded along in those hypnotic rhythms, exhausting the senses and letting creativity surface. We freed the
subconscious from its imprisonment in the mundane external world. We moved toward the source.

Nature entered their lives. The wilderness tracks of our
Blackwater Adventure Run territory were having their

effects. "I feel the trees," said Madeline. "There's a serenity there, no doubt about that," said George.

Jeri Carlson had lost forty pounds.

Each time we worked out, we penetrated deeper into the Blackwater wilderness. This was as much psychological as physical work. I did not want the group to become familiar with the obstacle course ahead, however. The unknown is an essential ingredient in making contact with the source. Instead we made a series of outward journeys in which the wilderness environment interacted with their senses of personal discovery, as flabby muscles strengthened and vascular and respiratory systems got into shape. They needed me as their goad to conscience, the fortifier of resolve through their contemplation of my own history. But by the day of the run, they would need nothing except themselves. So went my theory.

Each runner was entering his or her own myth, through which each might find a new way to live. Myths generate energy. Almost all are rooted in the earth and waters. We have to be able to trust them. We must be able to say that we created them and then made them believable, or sensible, to others.

The wilderness of the Blackwater was tiny, almost a pseudowilderness. Within it the performers, the actors in this small drama, were busily manufacturing myth. The mythmaker goes into the wilderness to find truth. He returns in heroic possession of something that changed him. Then it is time for others to learn what he has discovered.

Every myth makes it plain, too, that the wilderness's greatest gift is the return of the traveler to himself. The American writer and sports philosopher George Leonard, who wrote *The Ultimate Athlete*, says there is an athlete lurking inside every person. I did not need to do anything more than let the Blackwater people discover that they were runners.

As expected, each member of the group began to experience a split within him- or herself, one side remaining who they had been and the other side becoming what they were doing. This tension made them animated, excited, intense, alive.

Victor had given up smoking, even though a small paunch hung on. "I'll get to the beer and the food later," he puffed.

John's depression was changing, characteristically, to a feeling of pervasive fear. "What's going on?" he would ask apprehensively, as we entered another wilderness territory.

Madeline became very strong and a fast runner. She so outdistanced the others that they struggled to her pace to keep mastery over themselves. At the halfway point in training all of them were almost equally split between their old lives and the new one developing.

There was, therefore, great conflict and inner stress for each runner at this watershed in his or her personal transformation. To effect change in their lives, we had withdrawn from the patterns of the outside world. We were withdrawing each time we put ourselves deeper and deeper into the Blackwater. As the group's concern for the conventional world narrowed, invasions of the subconscious became everyday occurrences. Their dreams were changing, becoming significant, in the same way as their running was changing, the muscles appearing on their legs.

The surges of energy were beginning. These would be dangerous until the neophyte runners became fitter than they were. George wanted to trial-run a marathon at the end of the second week. Janet wondered whether she should start swimming, too, because she had been a fair swimmer in her childhood; the seduction of her present physical competence was working on her. I warned everybody about the dangers of being overambitious, of attempting to do more than they were in condition to do.

Perhaps Rousseau had been right. The "perfect" human being waited inside the imperfect body, the conflict-ridden mind, awaiting release. George Leonard had postulated the ultimate athlete, a child of nature, inside everyone. The Blackwater Adventure runners had dreams of themselves as better people; they were both dreaming of and striving for this image of perfection.

"I feel so alive!" said Madeline.

"I feel so frightened," said George.

"How can you stand it?" John asked him.

"Because it's a totally new experience," George replied.

This sense of discovery was exhilarating—the feeling that there might be immense, perhaps frightening, reserves of power lying hidden within each person. The Earth Adventures had shown how the devil is the self in a bewildering variety of disguises. Failure is always orchestrated from within. We sit within the powerhouse of self, whimpering about our incompetence, weakness, lack of desire; frightened to let out our creativity lest we discover ourselves. The Blackwater experience brought each participant to the point where he or she could risk being alone and competent, and so competing only on an internal level.

As the day of the televised run approached, a mysterious contagion grew within the group, the "catching fire" that New York Knicks player (and now United States Senator) Bill Bradley once described. It is the moment of the perfect Bradshaw throw connecting, a time when the whole body bursts "with happiness" in that ever-present possibility of the magical click occurring, when a completely new kind of reality suddenly grips all the participants. It is "this higher level of existence," says Michael Novak in his *Joy of Sports*. It is, of course, the energy of the source, flowing wild.

On the day before the run some of the participants were clearly showing signs of being in touch with the source. "I have this marvelous feeling of total freedom," said Janet McCluskey.

The next day six camera crews came from the television station to cover the run from various places along its ten-mile length. We gathered to talk. I told the television audience that we were like Zen archers, not trying to hit any target but seeking to create a perfect mental attitude in which we could run well.

"Are you all ready?" I cried. The group began limbering up. "We're going to get stretched out, warmed up, so we don't hurt ourselves."

Then to the audience I said, "This is an event that combines a sense of adventure with a challenge to mind and body. The challenge is to go beyond one's previously set limits. The point is to enjoy one's physical self and develop an increased awareness in the natural world. I believe that contact with the wilderness is a necessity for our survival, whether we walk, or run, or climb in it. We need it for our sanity.

"These men and women here today are people like ourselves who have something to overcome. Whether suffering from a sedentary lifestyle, lack of motivation, personal crisis, depression, or weight problems, all these people have one thing in common: they accepted the challenge to try something new—an adventure run. So let's cheer them on."

The camera revealed a group that still did not look close to marathon material. Victor Anselm had not dropped all of his paunch, and it bobbed up and down as he started to run. He had lost thirty-five pounds, though. The cameras revealed that he was knock-kneed, which none of us had noticed before.

"I've got to keep from falling," he kept saying to himself. "If I fall, then I'll be too frightened to run again. I know that from the fall I took on my bicycle when I was a kid." Like most of the Blackwater runners he was a victim of childhood hangups, fears he had not succeeded in outgrowing.

George Sutherland got across the first obstacle, a stream, but the steep bank on the other side stymied him. "My God," he said to himself, "I can't do it, and I'm on television."

At that, Janet McCluskey splashed up behind him and started clawing at the clay sides of the bank. She got a fingerhold and hauled desperately. George heaved a sigh and went up the bank like a cat, reaching the top almost before she did. Stress sent him pounding away into the woods, where, unwary now, he tripped on a vine and disappeared into a thicket with a howl. Janet passed him at a steady trot.

"Behind the curtain of our imperfections there lies the geometry of humming strings," says George Leonard.

But in the escape from imperfection, the fool may kill himself. The transition from helplessness to some degree of competence can also be a step toward self-destruction. The runner is a finely tuned machine, functioning more intensely than his lethargic peers.

"I've got to keep my legs going," said John Dolger, "and I have to think pleasant thoughts. I've got to keep my thinking good."

Each contestant had a different internal dialogue. Madeline Smith fell at Dinosaur Pond. When she got out of the water, she was saying to herself, "To think this is the way they settled America. My blisters have blisters!"

When Madeline came to a cliff beyond the pond, her will failed for a moment. She sat down, but nobody paid attention to her. The other runners passed her one by one. A television cameraman aimed his camera at her. She looked startled and got up.

The different challenges of the Blackwater course were designed to take the runners by surprise. Just as Jeri Carlson had become accustomed to slogging across an ancient cornfield, she suddenly found herself in three feet of water and forcing her way to the sandy shore on the other side. Just as Victor Anselm was beginning to feel he was getting his second wind, he encountered the long stretch of Apache Pass, or the Little Grand Canyon, to name just a couple of the obstacles to be surmounted. The running was designed

Blackwater runners scouting the early part of the course.
BILL HINTON.

to steal up on them, so that at the end they had done something their minds had told them was impossible.

Zen master Eugene Herrigel describes his success as an archer in *Zen and the Art of Archery.* "The shot will only go smoothly," he says, "when it takes the archer himself by surprise. You mustn't open the right hand on purpose." Many boxers have reported throwing winning punches without being aware that their fists, or even their arms, had moved at all. Each stood there looking down on his fallen opponent, wondering how he had gotten there.

"You become the wind," says Mike Spino, a thinking runner who wrote *Beyond Jogging.*

The longer the Blackwater Adventure Run continued, the more past hangups and conflicts disappeared. The effect might be only temporary, but it would be remembered. "When you've seen the light at the end of the tunnel, you must travel that tunnel," George Sutherland had said.

Each challenge along the way evoked a different kind of response. Some of the group were good runners but not climbers. The climbers were not necessarily the agile ones. Methodical and determined, they achieved by not being set back by any barrier. Their conquest of gravity was like conquering those weaknesses in themselves that had to be overcome.

Scrambling up and down the little Blackwater ravines was not like scaling mountains, of course, but they were climbs of a sort, Matterhorns in miniature to runners who were grateful merely to run on level ground.

"Like the pilot or the skier," said the great French mountaineer Louis Lachenal, "a man feels freed from the condition of the crawling bug and becomes a chamois, a squirrel, almost a bird."

The group ran on dirt road and rocky track, through a cornfield and the forest understory; they were scratched in the thick pine forest and mired in the wastes of an abandoned and rutted field. Madeline Smith later said, "Here, for the first time, I saw that there was a mountain to climb, a log to pass over, a stream to ford, and I wasn't sure that I could do it. It was all terribly real. And I was scared."

Fear cannot be avoided in the healing wilderness. In fact, risk, danger, and fear of the unknown are the stimuli to creative action. Dr. Sol Roy Rosenthal of the University of Illinois believes that exercise incorporating risk is vital to bodily conditioning and health. Fear is not a negative emotion. The avoidance of fear is not constructive, but the passing beyond it is. Jeri Carlson had come seven miles, and she looked good to finish now, a fat person no longer. John Dolger might look like a duck as he crossed a puddle, but he also looked strangely calm as he pounded along, hardly sweating anymore.

By running together the Blackwater contestants faced the fear of being left behind. None of them really knew, though, as they stumbled, falling and lurching into yet another ravine, that they were subject to the constant counseling of the environment around them. They were caught in the same kind of phenomenal relationship to nature as when a person is meditating. They were cut off from the conventional stimulations of the outside world. After an hour none of them paid any attention to the television cameras. They simply did not care about them anymore. The reality was not their appearance on the tube; it was goading their bodies to finish. They could feel only their pounding hearts and their screaming muscles while, outside of them, passing in a steady parade, were the comforting and beautiful images of wilderness forestlands. They were being hypnotized by the wilderness but also transformed by it.

Bruce Ogilvie, a psychologist at San Jose State University in California, made a study of athletic champions and discovered that athletes who gave everything they had were more stable personalities than those who did not try so hard. Furthermore, the riskier the sport, he found, the more solid the performer. Grand Prix drivers and sport parachutists, oddly enough, are more stable personalities than those in less challenging fields.

The Blackwater Adventure runners, coming now to the end of the two-hour course, might be a long way from jumping from airplanes for fun, but they were as much at their limits as any Grand Prix driver. They were extending themselves to what Ogilvie calls the "absolute physical, emotional and intellectual limits" of effort. Like it or not, they all would be changed at the end of this run.

Two Purdue University researchers, A. H. Ishmail and L. E. Trachtman, had tested middle-aged men at the start of a jogging routine and again months later. Uniformly they found that the discipline of the men's running and the stress of their efforts had actually changed their personalities. Suppressed capabilities came to the fore. The men showed greater decisiveness, were mentally more stable, had a sense of increased self-sufficiency, and, most surprisingly, all showed growth in imagination.

I ran ahead to the finish so that I could watch my people

coming in. I was surprised to see Madeline Smith close to the front, coming down a sandy bank. She looked very winsome as she trotted out of the shadows and onto the track leading to the finish line, and she was smiling. Then she was crying. Then she slumped down at the finish line. A moment later she was laughing.

Then came Jeri. She seemed to have lost more weight during the run. She wasn't going to cry for anybody. This was her biggest triumph. She would talk about it for years.

George was running through the distant trees, shouting. It sounded as though he were having some kind of fit. But he had seen the finish line, and he was wild with joy. He came galloping down the slope; but then, instead of crossing the stream completely, he turned midway and started running upstream, throwing up his arms and shouting, until the water got too deep for him to run and he threw himself face forward into the stream.

I ran down the slope toward him as Victor—who, I swear, seemed to have lost the rest of his paunch—also came down the slope. He too was on this high and did not even attempt to cross the stream, but just hurled himself into the water in a kind of racing dive. John was next, and then Janet, and then I was in the water, too, and we were all laughing and giggling and crying and splashing each other. Later none of them could remember whether the television cameramen were there or not.

The only way we could find out what the outside world had seen of the run was to watch the television show when it was broadcast. We arranged to do this together. As we sat there watching, we all were struck by the same thunderbolt at the same time.

"My God, there we are, doing it!" shouted Victor.

There they were—acting it, living it, running it.

The rest of the world was just watching it.

Chapter 9

The Wanderobo Wilderness

When I leaned back against the post of the dung-walled hut in the Wanderobo *manyatta*, or village, in central Kenya, my shoulder touched that of the *moran*, or warrior, next to me. Other figures were dimly visible in the gloom of the hut. Then a woman, Nebigili, blew on a coal and made a flame leap up. Suddenly I could see there were now more than a dozen people in the one-room loaf-shaped structure.

Lambat, my new-found Wanderobo friend, had introduced me to Nebigili, his wife, and Ngoto, his father. Now we were going to eat. Nebigili did the cooking with her right arm as she breast-fed the baby in her left. She poured water from a gourd into an earthenware pot to make coffee, took a piece of kindling from the fire, blew on it to make a tiny torch, and peered into the water. Before the room fell back into darkness, I saw her scoop out some bugs from the pot. Nearby, insects scurried up the walls.

These people were the Wanderobo, one of the so-called "running" peoples of East Africa—tall, lean men and women with aquiline noses, graceful body postures, and the speed of the wind in their feet. (They are also called the "Derobo," notably by Hemingway in *The Snows of Kilimanjaro*, but their true name for themselves is "Okiek.") Unlike their

177

neighbors, the cattle-herding Masai, the Wanderobo were primarily hunters. They were connected to their place on the earth by millennia of custom. I had become determined to share their lives and, perhaps, if I were lucky, to run through the land where they hunted.

Lambat had said that he might run with me. But what for? He could not understand running for the sake of running. I told him he could pretend he was hunting with me, searching out the game. He smiled at that. The *bwana* from America had strange ideas.

Anthropologists have said that high-speed bipedal human motion probably was born in the uplands of East Africa, in Kenya and Tanzania. Certainly these windswept thornbush and acacia highlands are ideal for running of any kind. They are open, yet attractively patched with trees, thickets of shrubs, swamps, and long-grass meadows, and are cut by infrequent, murmurous rivers. Many world champion athletes, including Kip Keino, Ben Jipso, Philbert Bayii and Henry Rono, had trained to success in this kind of country. In a proposal to a magazine for an article about a running safari, I had said, "Running man originated in East Africa, and I am going to run in his tracks."

Here also was the last great animal paradise on earth, nearly two million zebra, wildebeest, gazelle, and other large mammals crammed into an area smaller than the state of Maryland. A running man might feel as though he were in a Garden of Eden here, making a connection with some race memory in himself. In such a place prehistoric energies might be re-experienced.

The *moran* began to chant. The flickering fire revealed a row of them moving with the rhythmic beat, as they imitated the explosive coughs of lions. The atmosphere in the *manyatta* became intense. Before I slept that night, I knew how primitive men must have behaved before they went out in running pursuit of their game. I knew, too, that I would run with Lambat.

Jump dancing with a Wanderobo moran. The dance is a pre-hunt ritual meant to work the warriors up to a fever pitch. BILL EPPERIDGE.

David running near Naibor Keju. BILL EPPERIDGE.

Lambat worked as a tracker for Bill Winter, a hunter and safari organizer. A month earlier Bill had told me that he was planning to make a campsite on the slopes of Naibor Keju—White Legs Mountain—some 100 miles from the Wanderobo village, in the territory of the Samburu. "You can run from there," he suggested. "It's good open country, and you should not be bothered too much by thorns."

To reach the mountain was a short safari, and the sights, smells, and sounds of Africa were all around me. In one village, warriors strutted through the mud streets in their brilliant red togas—*shukas*—and looked at me as though I were subhuman. In another village, tall, fierce-looking Samburu men were decked out in beads and draped in red calico from chest to knee. Their hair was braided and painted with red ocher, and cross sections of hollowed elephant ivory gleamed in each gaping earlobe. Each carried a spear in his right hand. These were dancing men who could also run like deer.

I bought a throwing stick, called a *rungu*. About eighteen inches long, hewn from a branch of a thorn tree, it was intended for self-defense as well as hunting. The handle was slender but stiff, and the heavy end terminated in a knob. Lambat nodded when he saw it. "Good for games," he said.

At Naibor Keju we played with the *rungu*. I threw it experimentally, for distance. Lambat ran after it, then turned like a baseball player, wound up, and unleashed it straight for my head. His eyes shone with a wild, intense fire. I was the target. I rifled it back to him but just over his head. He fielded it, and back it came like a buzzing missile, straight for my chin. I whirred it right back at his breastbone, and he leaped aside a millisecond before it struck him.

The following day, without warning, Lambat said, "We run." He disappeared to change out of the khaki clothes he wore for his tracker's job. I had picked out a rough route for the run, but Lambat would set the pace and warn me of dangers. I trusted his intimate knowledge of the country. It was then four in the afternoon—the best time, he had said, to see the animals. The sporadic seasonal rains had started, and new grass was sprouting for as far as the eye could see. The animals were on the move. They grazed as they walked, but their real objective was the short-grass plains many miles away, where no tree or hill or river bed gave shelter to their enemies—the lions, leopards, hyenas, and wild dogs.

I changed into running shorts and shoes, hefted a spear in my right hand and the *rungu* in my left, and began warming up. Lambat appeared, dressed in his togalike *shuka* and wearing sandals, and without a word we set off. Naibor Keju rose wet and gleaming above us, pink stone in the saffron light of sun past its meridian. Baboons barked down at us from the glowing heights of granite cliffs.

We ran slowly and steadily, threading our way down rutted game trails. It had rained heavily in the night, and red mud made the footing treacherous. This was the kind of country, I knew, where we might come across a pride of lions sprawled out in the long grasses, sleeping off a big meal. Or the scattered trees might half-conceal a family

Role reversal: Lambat photographs David. BILL EPPERIDGE.

group of elephants. Or tall swamp grasses might suddenly disgorge the bad-tempered and highly dangerous cape buffalo.

I was apprehensive about stepping on one of the thick thorns that often lay scattered across our path. But Lambat either ignored them or had a sixth sense for avoiding them. We moved down a slope toward a half-dried waterhole, surrounded by the metallic sounds of flappet larks clacking their wings together.

As we passed the waterhole, tick birds flew up in a swarm, and a small crocodile silently submerged itself in a green scum. I let myself sink into the landscape, merge with the lean, black form flowing along beside me. Running alone is one thing. But running with Lambat was to remember that the purpose of fleetness of foot was either to escape danger or to run down something that was wanted. Lambat ran as his ancestors had run, without questioning the cost of the effort. The environment itself dictated the organization of effort to be without conflict, a reflex.

Here I felt both the simplicity and the discipline of the flow of natural energy. We were running with the earth itself. Nature loved us. The structuring powers of the super-ego that waited to slow the feet, unstring the muscles with lassitude, and even injure the runner who was not in touch with himself, were weaker here.

The links with the "soul of the universe," as Joseph Campbell describes it, were strong. I was connected through Lambat to something that was larger than anything I could see or know. We had run five miles into a wilderness of acacia and thornbush. We had passed out of the rainfall area of the previous night. Now we ran in dust along a winding, green-stained, dry stream bed, past termite mounds like brown wounds on the earth. The rhythm of running was like a metronome, a gathering in the unconscious. Inhibitions and restraints were dropping away. As usual, I felt as though I were falling but not in hazard; rather, into a deeper state of consciousness wherein lay the flow of the source.

Lambat's purplish black cheeks were streaked and runneled by sweat through the dust kicked up by our pounding feet. I wondered what was in his mind. Did he think I was mad? Was he running with me just to humor a white man from America?

I did not think so. He ran because he had some sense of what I was trying to do. He understood about the disciplining of self to the task, even though he might laugh at what I called work. When he sped the *rungu* at my brain, he was laughing. There was no hypocrisy or illusion between Lambat and the place where he lived.

To know oneself it is necessary to perceive identity and action in a relationship—here, my relationship with a primeval world and a man who resided in it. I had watched schizophrenics falling into their pits of despair while I remained safe on my firm ground. But my relationships with them had changed my own perception of where I stood.

Running in this place, I was split between the two worlds of the primitive and the civilized. Rosalind LaRoche had rejected the concept of the split in personality, but the patients at Earth House had talked for hours about that. "I am going into being two people," Barbara had said, "and one is an animal and the other is a plant." The other schizophrenics had all laughed at her, but reflected in that contrasting image was the conflict of their existence—they were not one thing or the other.

The schizophrenic plunges into the pit and so, temporarily, does the runner. There are times when athletes think they are going crazy. I remembered the hallucinations during long-distance swims, the out-of-body views of self. The athlete is always split, dressed in two raiments: a business suit in one guise, a track suit in the other. He is in the city. He wants to be in the wilderness. When I tried to get sponsors for an athletic event in North Africa, seeking the support of various New York business concerns, the corporate executives were more interested in learning about my wilderness experiences than in schemes to promote their products.

We thumped down a long incline of scattered shrubs, from which a bush pig ran grunting, and entered the dried-out bed of an extinct river. Of course, I could understand now that in order to make changes in life, one has to acknowledge a basic failure of self. Alcoholics cannot be cured until they are able to see themselves as alcoholics. Schizophrenics cannot begin cures until they admit that they are dysfunctional.

The athlete cannot reach a peak of effort until he is drained of his repressions and prejudices, the weight of his personal history. His feeling of falling comes at the time when the chemical reactions that sustain intense effort are literally burned out. It is a freeing of the system from hang-up and hangover. He is falling, only to get up afresh.

For many, perhaps, and especially for me, taking the plunge flushes creativity into the consciousness. It is a moment of both confusion and ecstasy. If the unconscious is truly ready for the mighty plunge, then it may be experienced with joy and expectation. Sublime delights reside in that realm, replenishing, revealing, reviving, and, of course, healing. The Golden Gate feeling.

But if, as Jung describes it, there is nothing in the unconscious except "disposable libido," just floating around in a vortex of artificial stimuli, then the individual is in for a bad time. Drugs, alcohol, and material acquisitions become the lifelines, convenient medicines for a torment that seemingly cannot be treated in better ways.

I had an image of an underground river flowing beneath the green bed of the dead watercourse we were crossing. But how to deal with a psychic underground river if its flow is out of conscious control? If it is the power of universal action and carries all with it, what might be the individual's connection to it?

Joseph Campbell calls such awareness the "classical period" of perception. Both the runner in his track suit and the overweight, sedentary worker in his office tower might look outward and ask why they are on the earth. Only the one who is connected to the underground flow will have an answer. Lambat had the answer: a man in his place, his identity unambiguous.

I looked back at my—our—doubts in identity. It is easier to suppress such doubts than to face them. But if they are suppressed, they just lie low and wait. When the light of a person's life begins to descend—to take the plunge, perhaps—they will be met on the way down. Then a man may be forced to decide whether a San Francisco bar, pretty girls, and a convertible are the real reasons for being on earth.

We floated through the original zoo. Animals trudged everywhere in search of what they needed. At times they were almost oblivious to us. We bisected herds of wildebeest and sent zebras flaring away in a stammer of hoofsteps. We were joined in a common language of action. I thought about the Pioneer people, who had done the same kind of thing. The students at Earth House moved toward cures by acting first and thinking afterward. The animals know to move to the plain just before the rains bring forth its succulent short grass. We knew to run before it was preached by the gurus of well-being.

I looked across at Lambat's streaked face, and he half-smiled. The flow was carrying him forward, too. I wondered how it ran through him. For me it came rising from the subconscious, where madness and creativity precariously coexist. This is no logical state. We create ourselves with each step we take. We might be going backward and forward simultaneously. We might race in time as well as in space, heading toward both death and the place where the infant dwells. I understood then how the psychotic becomes as a child, or even a fetus in the womb. The Greeks, with their profound knowledge of psychology, went even further; they portrayed Daphne turned into a tree as they sought to describe the psychotic condition, the downward plunge.

All right, I said to myself, in the transformed state, the runner might be mad. He is beyond himself, running his demons to exhaustion instead of trying to outdistance them. Daphne could not handle her feelings of sexuality. They could not be examined, or left behind. This left her frigid to the seduction of the god Apollo. But he was mad for her and saw in that trembling virgin the personification of a dream. She could not stand such pressure. She cried out for help.

"Father!" she screamed.

In crisis, the people of Earth House always cried out for those who had created them, their parents. Daphne's cry was for the river god, Peneus. The great internal flow of the self was, indeed, a river. Peneus faced the prospect of seeing his daughter go mad, or die, with feelings she could not handle. He saved her life, at least, by turning her into a tree.

Lambat and David on the trail. BILL EPPERIDGE.

In our running we had elected to make our bodies feel. We were alive! We passed under a grove of acacias. If we felt pain, it was our own, and we had control over it. We could stop. "Look," said Lambat, pointing ahead with a quick gesture. I saw another grove of acacias, those graceful, flat-topped trees that seem to line every horizon of this beautiful East African landscape. But instead of being green and pale and feathery, they were as dark as a thundercloud and swarming with movement, as if infested with insects. Then I could see that they were filled with birds, millions of birds.

They were a certain kind of grass finch that periodically swarms down from the northern countries—the Sudan and Ethiopia—to these savannas in search of food and places to breed. They are a plague, hated by both Africans and Europeans, because when they descend on farms they eat everything they can find. As we came closer, the birds started to leave the trees, and the blue sky darkened with their departure.

By the time we reached the acacias, the trees were empty and silent. No other bird or insect or animal could have coexisted in the trees with such an enormous swarm. I felt as though I were coming into a big railroad station that, only a moment before, seen from a high balcony, had been teeming with people hurrying toward different tracks. But now, with all the trains gone, it was abandoned.

Running, I once wrote in a magazine article, is a moving meditation. It is a reaching for a kind of eternity where the euphoric state of extended effort will become permanent. It is meditation that does not separate itself from the physical world, but demands the concrete skills of not falling down, of coordinating limbs and eyes, of pacing one's energy and determination against distance, time, and feeling.

At an ashram in India I had read a line in the *Bhagavad-Gita* that reminded me of the feeling of eternity the long-distance runner gets when he has run beyond himself into the world of the source. "Never is it born, never does it die. . . . Unborn, eternal, permanent, and primeval, it is not slain when the body is slain."

Running as a means of reaching a spiritual state is well enough known today. "When one completely withdraws the senses from their objects, then is one's wisdom fairly fixed. In that serenity is surcease of all sorrow." The *Bhagavad-Gita* is explicit about the source, and its writers knew the power of concentrating all effort on a limited objective, as I now concentrated every faculty I possessed on avoiding a sudden scattering of thorns in the grasses under my feet.

We were approaching the ninety-minute mark. This signaled a change in the rhythm of my effort, a point when the hypnosis of pain and exhaustion is starting to exert its effects on the conscious mind. Sometimes there is a sensation of drowning. But there is also an expectation of breaking through to more solid country beyond.

Lambat was suffering now, but he would not show me that. We were bonded to the landscape that floated past us—these lions and impala, these zebras and warthogs and remote eagles. This was the very unity of nature that I had experienced in the Sierra as a youngster. It was the reason why I ran now and was in this place. Within the feeling produced by it, everything was known and was in its place and had significance. It was the morality of nature that Emerson talked about. There was an ethical spirit within the embrace of nature.

For Lambat this was nothing to discuss, because it was his life. Lambat came from stock that thought nothing of running for half a day if necessary. The hunter gets his kick in the hunt, obviously, when the great run ends in the kill. This has been ritualized by all the hunting peoples. The blood of the victim is also the pain of the hunter's effort to kill, the patience and dedication and concentration necessary to bring the prey down. At the moment of the kill the hunter feels regret, because in such ardent pursuit he must identify with his victim and so feel loss when the object of his concentration dies.

Lambat's *rungu* speeding toward my head had spoken of a darker and more complex sense of self. We are killers. The lions we ran among had a different sense of themselves than did the antelope they ate. The herbivorous antelope could not have any feeling about killing something.

I had been struck in my experiences at Earth House by how vivid was the schizophrenics' notion of death as a presence in life. They had experienced the revelation of death within their own sufferings. I understood now, perhaps as a result of the exaggerated recall common in marathon effort, that this encounter might be a very deep and perhaps destructive experience. In making a supreme effort, it might be necessary to concentrate on meeting one's own soul, my Greek daimon and my Egyptian healer, those spirits that are my guardians and my friends as well as my most ingenious and deadly enemies.

There are accounts of this phenomenal experience. The

Golden Gate episode was my introduction to it. The first Pillars of Hercules swim had been the negative side of it. So, the place of revelation might be filled with gods and powerful spirits, angels. But it also might be crammed with devils and a phalanx of shattering forces, as the schizophrenics revealed.

If the traveler overcomes the drowning sensation or does not yield to its panic, then he or she moves into a series of rapid climaxes—"overwhelming crises," as one man described them—each one greater than the last, until the mind cannot stand it and either snaps or flees. The successful runner, like Roger Bannister striving for the ultimate effort of the first four-minute mile, passes out.

This is creative breakdown. It is also the plunge of the schizophrenic into real insanity, involuntary breakdown. No schizophrenic in my experience ever recovered without many preliminary breakdowns. Only in breakdown, in the plunge, might the demonic self be confronted, the difficulty resolved. But facing this oblivion requires a heroic effort.

We were at the halfway point of the run, just a little short of two hours from the camp, with Naibor Keju on our right as we circled around a swamp of tall grasses; crowned cranes and a group of vultures watched us from a dead baobab tree. The return journey would be the test and resolution of the run. Joseph Campbell is eloquent about the journey of the mythical hero:

A person who in childhood has been deprived of essential love, brought up in a home of little, or no care, but only authority, rigor, and commands, or in a house of tumult, and wrath, a drunken father raging about, or the like, will have been seeking in his backward voyage a reorientation and centering of his life in love.

Stomach cramps came and went.

Accordingly, the culmination (when he will have broken back to the start of his biography, and even beyond, to a sense of the erotic first impulse to life) will be a discovery of a center in his own heart of tenderness and of love in which he can rest. That will have been the aim and meaning of his entire backward quest. And its realization will be represented through an experience, one way or another, of some sort of visionary fulfillment of a "sacred union" with a wifely, mothering (or simply a mothering) presence.

I ran blindly, automatically, awaiting the last great infusion of energy that would get me home.

It is a lack of such energy for the return journey that fells the schizophrenics. They cannot get up. "Help me, help me." Sane, healthy people cannot function without the energy of homecoming. It is essential to make the return journey, which is the hardest task. Campbell says the loss of energy, the fall, might be caused by a father who has been a nonpresence, without authority or influence or anything that can be honored or respected. Then the plunge is directed toward seeking the father image, to some "sort of symbolic realization of supernatural daughterhood, or sonship to a father."

Beyond the second hour Lambat strengthened, and I could feel the so-called "second wind" possessing me. William James called it finding "the vital reserves" that can be reached only by pushing beyond the apparent limits of endurance. Beyond, perhaps, there is limitless perception, boundless energy; the source is in charge. I had run with the Tarahumara Indians in Mexico's Sierra Madre; these Indians run for twenty-four hours just for the fun of it. Who knew the limits, or if there were any?

The dust boiled up from under our feet and coated our forearms. I felt it congealing on my face. The plunge, this great interior acceleration, is always for a reason. It is the centerpiece of the healing journey. Indian hunters would sleep for two days after running down forest deer in chases that lasted for perhaps forty hours. Breakdown is not a disgrace but a release. The runner "breaks down" when his apparent endurance is reached. But usually he can recover by restructuring his attitude toward the race or the destination or the meaning of his traveling, and thus reach the hidden reserves and continue. Again, the healing process, the old perception left behind, the new and changed territory opened up.

It is a plain matter of putting more into it to get more out of it, a truth of proverbial simplicity. But like all great truths it is so close it appears to be invisible, inside the range of normal focusing. But its inaccessibility is also its compelling beauty. Of course, there must be the most frightful fear in such a journey. There has to be a guardian at the gate of paradise, or else everybody would get in, and it would not be paradise. I wondered how many were willing to pay the price, in fear, of the entry.

R. D. Laing, the Scottish psychoanalyst, describes a fall of self at the midpoint of a journey, when forward motion cannot be maintained and there is no energy to return home. A British naval officer who was also an artist suffered a schizophrenic breakdown. But perhaps because of his service discipline, he was able to go a very great distance into the experience in a lucid condition and to return with a report.

He was hit by the classical blinding light experience, which is the Buddha light described in the Tibetan *Book of the Dead*. This is supposed to occur at the time of death. If it can be endured, then a renaissance occurs, and the terrible pain of rebirth is experienced.

The naval officer went into a ten-day voyage of breakdown, or breakup. He entered the frightening experience of backward-running time (a manifestation of the plunge), accompanied by the uncanny feelings of having died, of falling, of wandering into wild animal landscapes where all else was traveling but he himself was bound and still. He felt himself turning into a baby and heard himself cry. But he also felt great new powers of controlling his body and of having immense influence over others. Like the Indian *siddhi*, which I had learned about after the first Gibraltar swim, this is actually a consciousness of powers that are in all of us.

The search for the real self is the reason for the hero's journey and why, in this grandiose spectacle of natural history, it was necessary for me to run instead of merely to watch. If I had the patience to watch with the same intensity as I ran, I would achieve the same effect. In the end it must be a spiritual experience.

The Bible describes the achievement of spiritual revelation through journeys made in the skies, in the waters, or upon the earth. The slopes of the biblical mountain invite souls to climb toward the heavenly state. Climbing, whether literal or metaphoric, is exhausting and can induce a suggestible state, as in distance running a form of self-hypnosis is produced by exhaustion and the pounding rhythms of the feet. Then it is possible to feel the presence of invisible gods, waiting on the higher plane and encouraging the hero onward and upward. These gods, says Campbell, "are in charge and running things: and in the highest place, the highest job, was the highest god of all."

We flew into the third hour, contact lost with my feet as a bulk of elephants merged into a dark clump of trees a mile away. My lungs, guts, and shoulders had become automatic appendages of the act of running. Here, too, the intensity of inner concentration, the hoot of a hyena and a posing of three cheetahs on a termite mound.

The naval officer began to realize, as his journey accelerated, that in the highest place lies madness—at least as this state is interpreted by a person who has not yet reached it. God Himself is a madman. The middle stages of the journey are through hell, which, as a part of the "awakening" process, is necessary before greater altitude is possible. The runner bears his "enormous load" of striving as a pure burden. There is no way of dodging the journey.

Lambat was reaching another climax as we hit the twenty-mile mark, going into the fourth hour. He had gone through his second wind and was exhausted at the next level, and although he could keep going, he had lost the power that had driven him at the beginning.

"Much pain," he said, faltering.

Now I felt the pain, too. It has been described as "a terrible joy," the blinding universal emotion, the coexistence of moving and stopping, of feeling and not feeling, of pain and pleasure. The British naval officer, who at the highest level of his journey was indeed mad, was also reaching the final confrontation. It had been a terrible test. He was bearing the full burden of his responsibility to it, the ultimate test of who he was.

"At times," he said, "it was so devastating that I'd be afraid of entering it again. . . . It was like a sudden blast of light, wind, or whatever you like to put it as, against you; so that you feel that you're too naked and alone to be able to withstand it."

Finally he'd had enough. He stopped taking the hospital sedatives. He sat on the edge of his hospital bed, clenched his hands together, and kept repeating his name over and over again as he sought to recover his identity. Suddenly it was finished, and he was sane again, but forever changed.

We came around a last group of acacias. Naibor Keju loomed against the red backdrop of evening sky. We passed the waterhole where we had seen the crocodile. Soon the camp came into view on the slopes of the mountain. Lambat was beat, but now he knew he could reach home without breaking down. He would not dishonor himself in the American's eyes—even if I would not have seen it as such. He was almost home.

Joseph Campbell followed the journey of Laing's British naval officer. "If one is to return home," he said,

one must not identify one's self with any of the figures or powers experienced. The Indian yogi, striving for release, identifies himself with the Light, and never returns. But no one with a will to the service of others, and of life, would permit himself such an escape. The ultimate aim of the quest, if one is to return, must be neither release nor ecstasy for oneself, but the wisdom and power to serve others. And there is a really great, as well as greatly celebrated, Occidental tale of such a round trip to the Region of Light, in the ten-year voyage of Homer's Odysseus—who, like the Royal Navy commodore, was a warrior returning from long battle years to domestic life, and required, therefore, to shift radically his psychological posture and center.

By the time we reached the camp, we were totally caked with dust. Some Samburu had wandered into the camp. They stood there like ebony statues, the crimson light of the almost-set sun washing their gleaming shoulders with natural paint. They looked fierce, but the next day I was playing Frisbee with them.

We sat by the campfire after rubbing ourselves down, and talked about Africa and what the future held. We said nothing about the run. My customary obsession to analyze and measure had deserted me. This was the time when the clock of consciousness was reset, so that it would run steadier in the unpredictable future.

I had some intimations. I felt in a constant state of nowness, moving, talking, laughing. I was, in fact, still running. I ran onward, erect and serene, in slow motion. Bill Winter told us about the time a safari client shot him by mistake, trying to save him from a cape buffalo that Winter had already killed. Lambat had changed back into his khaki shorts and shirt. I flowed on silently, the source beneath me.

Epilogue

Farther Down the Road

When I started my wilderness adventures in 1964, the idea that nature could heal was pretty far from mainstream consciousness. But today it is growing through an expanding network of efforts. Outward Bound programs test the fortitude and adaptability of young people to severe limits. Other wilderness programs and adventure travel tours take ordinary people to the tops of high mountains, the centers of bleak deserts, to the ends of the earth—largely in search of the kind of experience that is the backbone of this book. Countless self-improvement and self-healing programs, from EST to Hatha yoga, from Esalen to recent experiments in paroling criminals, seek to discover the great internal energy that everyone possesses and turn it toward positive and productive action.

Wilderness therapy, as it is now being called, is an established discipline. American social scientists recently set up the Wilderness Psychology Group as a national clearing-house of information on the subject and to share the results of specific research.

The late Dr. David Sheinkin, a physician in Westchester, New York, is one of many medical and scientific people who have studied the effects of wilderness on mind and body. "Wilderness," he once told me, "is most definitely a therapy, and very probably a medicine."

The eminent mythologist Joseph Campbell, whose *The Hero with a Thousand Faces* is known to thousands of college students and others, has said: "When you get sick, you lie down, rest, sleep. The body knows how to cure itself in all but the most serious illnesses. Nature knows best."

Thomas Stich, of the Dartmouth Medical School, uses rock climbing, canoeing, backpacking, and ski tours in wilderness areas as methods of therapy. "The outdoors provides us with tough challenges and opportunities for emotional growth that simply cannot be duplicated inside four walls," he is quoted as saying in a 1979 *New York Times* article.

The same article notes that the famed McLean Psychiatric facility at Massachusetts General Hospital also uses the "simplified environment" of the wilderness to treat patients. Therapists Pamela Hedrick and James Kahn conduct a program that begins with 30 days of physical training, after which the patients are taken into a wilderness environment in which they learn to trust themselves while also experiencing the values of interdependence—much like the Earth House approach.

Still another wilderness therapy program, called "Facing Fear Through Mountaineering," was recently featured in the *Los Angeles Times*:

> The program . . . was designed by Long Beach marriage and family counselor Michael Alvarez to use fear of the wilderness experience as a metaphor for life's more common stumbling blocks. "Learning field navigation with compasses and maps is like finding your way whenever you're lost," Alvarez said. . . . Leaning backwards into space secured only by one hand on a rope is like letting go of old beliefs."
> The end goal is not to overcome fear . . . but rather to become familiar enough with the process of coping to be able to use it again in other fearful situations.

Running in the Sahara, during the Everyman's Olympics.
LEE MARSHALL.

As for myself, I'm less inclined to risk my neck these days, and increasingly occupied with trying to communicate the benefits of wilderness therapy.* I do a lot of lecturing and demonstrating to university audiences, health conferences, and business and athletic groups. I helped to conceive and now act as consultant to an outdoor adventure program called "Survival of the Fittest" for NBC-TV SportsWorld. Much of my time currently is devoted to planning and organizing a new series of wilderness adventure-cum-therapy trips for average adults with a basic level of fitness and a strong sense of commitment to change and improvement. The locale will be the Caribbean, our magic carpets will be kayaks, and the elements will include fun, food-gathering, survival games, and a measure of healthy stress.

* I invite readers who have an interest in the field or information to share to write to me in care of Sierra Club Books, 2034 Fillmore Street, San Francisco, CA 94115.

More than anything else in the world, my father wanted me to graduate from Stanford with a medical degree. Instead I got kicked out of two colleges and finished none of my early studies. Through the years, I often asked myself why I was so tenacious in accomplishing physical exploits when I would not make the effort to finish a relatively simple liberal arts course.

Perhaps the answer to that question is summed up in this book. Pressure to make the individual conform is fine when it works, disastrous when it does not. For me, it is an issue of the age. I did not think I was dumb. And I knew from my reading and from talking to other athletes that physical activity and intellectual pursuits go very well together, even enhance each other. Eventually I began to feel that my own life demonstrated this.

In the spring of 1981, I graduated *summa cum laude* from the University of West Pensacola with a degree in communication arts. Returning to college with a specific goal in mind—learning communication skills—made all the difference for me. I went at my studies this time around in the same way I undertake wilderness adventures: as a focused, intense, compressed effort. I worked two straight years, summers included, and for one semester obtained special permission to take extra units. In other words, I invoked the same kind of stress—just enough to peak my performance but not enough to overtax my concentration—as I am used to in physical adventuring.

I didn't give up my wanderings entirely at this time, but my classwork gave them a new dimension. I became more aware of the subtle ways in which people of different cultures communicate—or fail to communicate—during a bicycle trip across the Andes Mountains of Peru and a marathon run over the Khyber Pass, that historic corridor linking Afghanistan and Pakistan. I was almost forced to give up the Khyber run, not because the hostile local tribesmen objected to my Western politics, but because my bare legs and floppy running shorts offended their sense of decorum.

Encounter with llamas, bicycle trip across the Andes.
JACK WRIGHT.

My college graduation took place just one month after my father died. The channels of communication between us two had long since been reopened, and I knew he was proud of me—not only for graduating at last but also for my less conventional achievements. And I had understood for some time what a wise man he had been. In a very different way from mine, his whole life had been an expression of what I had been trying to demonstrate: that nature is the best guide for both the human body and spirit, and that it would work for you if you would only let it.

Just before I got the news of his death, I was playing with my two kids, Daren and Chelsea. Daren wanted me to tell the story again of how I had swum Loch Ness in the hope of meeting the monster.

"It's never as bad as we think when we meet our monsters," I said.

"But she'd eat you all up," said Daren.

"She didn't, though," I said.